THE QUIET CRISIS

THE QUIET CRISIS

*How Higher Education
Is Failing America*

Peter Smith

California State University–Monterey Bay

ANKER PUBLISHING COMPANY, INC.
Bolton, Massachusetts

39.95

The Quiet Crisis
How Higher Education Is Failing America

ISBN 1-882982-70-3

Composition by Delaney Design
Cover design by Jennifer Arbaiza Graphic Design

Anker Publishing Company, Inc.
176 Ballville Road
P.O. Box 249
Bolton, MA 01740-0249 USA

www.ankerpub.com

DEDICATION

This book is dedicated to Sally, without whose friendship and great patience I could not have done the work of my life; to Brenda, whose steadfast support is the rock I rely on; and to all the learners who live in the shadows at the margins of American higher education. May we shine our light on them so they may be able to shine their light on us.

About the Author

Founding president of two institutions—the Community College of Vermont (1971) and California State University–Monterey Bay (1994)—Dr. Peter Smith has also served as vice president of advancement at Norwich University (1986) and dean of the Graduate School of Education and Human Development at George Washington University (1991). He has served on several boards, including the National Center for Higher Education Management Systems, Education Commission of the States, and the Council for Adult and Experiential Learning, and has chaired the Fund for the Improvement of Postsecondary Education. Smith also served as a member of the Carnegie Forum on Education and Economic Development (1985), as a senior fellow at the American Council on Education (1991), and as a member of the Wingspread Group on Higher Education (1993). Named Man of the Year by the National Council of Community Service and Continuing Education in 1976, he also received *Change* magazine's recognition as one of America's outstanding educators under the age of 40 in 1978. He has served as chair of his local school board, Senator in the Vermont State Senate, as lieutenant governor for Vermont, and as congressman-at-large for Vermont. He received his baccalaureate degree from Princeton University in history, magna cum laude, in 1968 and his master's and doctorate in administration, planning, and social policy from the Harvard Graduate School of Education in 1984. He lives in Marina, California, with Sally, his wife of 34 years.

TABLE OF CONTENTS

Preface

Forty years ago, while hiking in the Rockies as a student with the Colorado Outward Bound School, I fell in love with learning. It was a month that changed my life forever. I hiked, learning expeditioning skills and survival techniques with a diverse group of other young men. I reflected on the experience with daily diary entries. And I learned about teamwork firsthand as the group struggled to make its way from the Capitol Peak region to the Maroon Bells and back. My personal learning had two dimensions. First, my knowledge of backcountry expeditioning and the necessary skills from planning, to orienteering, to cooking, to rock climbing, to knots was deepened significantly. The course ended with a multi-day solo experience in which each student had to demonstrate his or her ability to survive in the wilderness. Second, however, was my behavioral learning. I learned about the strength of the team, about my own strengths and weaknesses in that situation, that everyone had a contribution to make, and the pitfalls of ignoring the team. So powerful was that experience I can still remember the names and faces of my tent-mates, fellow students, and leaders.

As I continued into and through college, my interest in learning deepened. However, as I began to consider a career in education, I was surprised and disappointed to discover that most schools and colleges did not share my passion. My own university was opposed to preparing undergraduates for careers in education and refused to assist several of us as we set up a mentoring program for urban school children—too "professional" they said. And my experience in graduate school was a continuation of the experience that I came to call the "shut up and listen" approach to teaching and learning. An early teaching internship was a near disaster as I struggled to teach high school seniors about whom I knew nothing. But I also remembered the professors who cared, the moments when personal attention mattered, and the points of enormous value within the larger experience.

And so, as a result of these and other experiences, as well as my own human nature, I have spent the last 35 years trying to create educational environments where learning and the needs of the learner lie at the center and are the core purposes of the operation, where personal learning and the pedagogies of teaching and learning are core values, not marginal concepts. As I walked along this path, I was fortunate to receive a Mina Shaughnessy Fellowship from the Fund for the Improvement of Postsecondary Education (FIPSE) in the early 1980s. Through the fellowship, I interviewed adult learners across the country in an attempt to tease out the impact of their experiential learning on their lives and the value of having it assessed for academic credit by colleges and universities. In simpler terms, I wanted to look at their learning outside of college, find out why they learned, how they learned, what they learned, and what impact that learning had on them. I was eager to see how the findings in my interviews stacked up against the research that I had read, my own professional experiences, and my gut feelings about learning.

The end result of the Shaughnessy Fellowship was a book, *Your Hidden Credentials: The Value of Learning Outside College* (1983). As the title suggests, *Your Hidden Credentials* made the case for the significance of learning that is gained experientially, outside of college, its assessment for academic credit, and its impact on individual human development. I believed then, and still do today, that ignoring this learning weakens the formal education we have to offer, frustrates and weakens the learner, and pushes huge lost opportunity costs onto the back of the larger society.

The Quiet Crisis: How Higher Education Is Failing America incorporates and builds on this earlier work. Twenty years have gone by and the negative consequences of our educational oversights are multiplying exponentially. *The Quiet Crisis* is more urgent and less gentle on the "education industry" and those who make our public policy than was *Your Hidden Credentials*. Our current record as "the best higher education system ever" isn't good enough for the world we live in. America is headed for a social, civic, and economic disaster if we are not successful in graduating a far higher percentage of our population from high school and college while bringing increasing numbers of working Americans back to finish their degrees.

The Quiet Crisis argues that we are failing to educate large numbers of students (of all ages) successfully because we are employing an out-of-date educational model that ignores the knowledge and resources available to make them successful. There is another story lying behind the consistent reports that our higher education system is the best ever, educating more students successfully than ever before. Although some individual institutions may show marginal improvement, when taken as a whole, American higher education is not on a success track to the future for American society.

The Quiet Crisis connects the dots of several separate, but associated phenomena to reveal the hidden crisis in American higher education and make recommendations for its transformation and improvement.

The picture that emerges is not a pretty one. It does not, however, lay the responsibility for the crisis on the learners, or their teachers, the usual whipping boys of educational criticism. Nor does it criticize K–12 education in order to protect the postsecondary sector, or vice versa. It says, clearly and forcefully, that our schools are organized for failure; that our historic "industrial model" simply won't make the grade in the 21st century. We are at a policy crossroads.

The Quiet Crisis is organized around three themes.

- **Our current "success" rates are confused, misleading, and misunderstood**. Race and income are still directly linked to success in higher education. Despite our best efforts to level the playing field while maintaining standards, American higher education still works disproportionately well for people who are Anglo and in the upper third of the country's income distribution. This is not news, but as a policy matter, it needs repeating. If your family is not in the upper

40% of income distribution and is a family of color (other than Asian-American), your prospects for success in college (to the BA) are severely limited. Yet, over 80% of our school population growth is projected to occur in the very income and ethnic sectors where we are currently falling short (Carnevale & Fry, 2002). Therefore, it is entirely possible that because of the current distribution of ethnicity and income, we will continue to have slightly improving success rates nationally for several years into the future as a higher percentage of Anglo students from the top 40% succeed in school. But if we fail to reach and succeed with the students of capacity from the other 60%, we will be sowing the seeds of larger failure within the reported success. Like corrosion hidden under a car's bumper, our failure within the success will be eating away at our social, civic, and economic infrastructure. We know that success in higher education is positively related to earnings, voting, and civic engagement. My conclusion: If we don't change our ways, our short-term success will lead to longer-term disaster.

- **Schools stifle learning.** The American higher education establishment largely ignores the science that already exists about how people learn best. We continue to substitute the traditional model of education for an informed, professionally based educational process. Our actions say that we are committed to a specific version of how to do business that is uninformed—structurally and professionally—by what we know about how people learn. As a result, millions of people of all incomes and races fail to thrive in our schools, not because they lack the capacity to learn, but because our schools and colleges lack the capacity to educate. In a world where we have insulin patches for diabetics, we ignore the science of learning, asking students and workers to "tough it out," to succeed or fail, based on their sheer will and effort. This attitude is as outrageous as it is unnecessary. America needs to organize its schools and colleges around what we already know about learning.

- **Technology is part of the solution.** Technology is transforming our capacity to support high-level learning anywhere, anytime, for anyone. The traditional academic model is based on outdated assumptions about the use of time, space, and responsibility. Technology changes all that, permitting radically different uses of time and space, and different allocations of responsibility that will allow for deeper and better learning for many more people when it is harnessed to support learning. It not only has the capacity to change the way we "instruct," but also the way we manage and support teaching and learning.

These three tenets are not news to any knowledgeable reader. We have studied them, discussed them, and written about them. But we haven't done anything about them. And for years, millions of parents have continued to wonder how a child who was inquisitive and bright at home could do so poorly in school. And for many, many students, school lay somewhere between being a necessary evil that was survived and a deception colored by personal failure that was not.

The Quiet Crisis explores the three themes' interaction on each other and the resulting dynamic change rippling through our society, including its requirements for success through education. Instead of investigating each issue vertically, I take the horizontal view, looking across them all and through the next 20 years, analyzing their interaction, their synergy, and their implications. My conclusion is that without major policy and organizational changes, our current "success" in higher education will evolve into a national crisis.

Part One describes the quiet crisis in American higher education. Drawing on my own experience as an educator and as a policymaker and using research data and stories, I paint the picture of our current situation, its strengths, its pitfalls, and its implications for the future. The message is clear: The promise of opportunity lies at the heart of our historic and future national success. And education is the gateway to opportunity. Yet much of the tradition of higher education, including the organizational model we employ, is exclusive, outdated, and ineffective. It won't get us where we need to go as a society. This is a challenge that reaches far beyond the current scope of our colleges and universities. Unless we rethink higher education profoundly, we will fail, slowly but inexorably, serving a declining percentage of the population successfully. Higher education must move from a position in American society that is justified by tradition to one that is characterized by value.

Part Two describes the new learning ethos that is emerging in America. Driven by three forces—demography, technological change, and new knowledge about how people learn—the new learning ethos lies beyond our educational institutions, in the larger society and the communities that surround them. These three forces, and the characteristics of formal or "supported" learning in the future, are discussed as value propositions in the new ethos for higher education.

In Chapter 4, Lived Experience: The Root of Learning, I describe how folklore and common sense are confirmed by research that people learn continuously and are changed by their learning. Excellent teaching and learning in the 21st century will build from the learner's experience and acknowledge the learning which experience generates. Chapter 5, Personal Learning, Reflection, and Growth, extends the discussion, exploring the relationships between assessment, reflection, and growth. Active reflection is the process through which the raw material of experience can be converted into learning. The relationship among experience, reflection, and conscious personal growth is described through three stories. And Chapter 6, Diversity: The Tie That Binds, describes ways to build in diversity at the core of the educational enterprise, treating it as an asset to be developed, not a deficit to be remediated. Finally, Chapter 7, From Wishes to Wireless, suggests some ways that technology connects, infuses, and drives the new learning ethos through its transformational impact.

Part Three: FutureThink, takes a look at what the future might look like. Prophecy is chancy stuff, and predictions are often wrong precisely because they try to anticipate dynamic change and describe its consequences. By its nature, dynamic change drives outcomes and creates conditions that were unimagined. Even so, if we don't try to imagine the future, we cannot begin to prepare the policies and practices that will support the diversified and dramatically reconceived teaching and learning of the future. Using vignettes, Part Three describes several versions of what learners and workers might experience in 2025, suggesting policies and initiatives that both encourage and support a new mainstream for postsecondary education.

Historically, colleges and universities have been able to pick and choose their structural reforms, adapting the institution to the reform over time while simultaneously re-making the reform through adaptation. But the diversity emerging in our society will neither wait nor delay in its emerging majority. The jobs we are creating and the needs for a more highly educated workforce will not wait for institutional redefinition. Nor will the changes in behavior and productivity coupled with a revolutionary redistribution of personal power and authority through the technology revolution be sidetracked while higher education decides what to do. And, if our colleges and universities do not start drawing on the knowledge about how people learn, our failures will continue to accumulate. These three tenets are societal forces driving change outside of our institutions that are changing the environment in which they operate. They are also, simultaneously, forces for change within our institutional walls.

The Quiet Crisis looks toward the future and describes why we must rethink the strategic vision, the structure, the calendar, and the way we practice higher education in America. There will be those who argue that I should have gone deeper into the demographic and persistence data than I have. And there will be those who wish I had been more complete in my description of the new science about learning. And still others will lament that I have failed to give sufficient weight to the technological revolution. My intention is not, however, to parallel others who know more about each of these areas. Nor is it to engage in either statistical or philosophical warfare. Rather, it is to give an urgent, commonsense policy perspective, from the ground level, about where we are headed and our capacity for transformational change.

This is an emergency made all the more critical by our complacent sense that all is well, that we are "the best," and that we're doing better every year. Such thinking is both arrogant and dangerous. We are the best. But all is not well and we are on the verge of succeeding our way to failure. I believe in outcomes. So, what are my hoped-for outcomes for you, the reader?

- First, I hope you will be able to identify and develop core elements essential to the effective transformation of higher education.

- Second, I hope you will be able to identify ways to promote the transformation of higher education, whether as a student, parent, educator, administrator, policymaker, or other interested party.

- Third, I hope you will reaffirm your conviction that higher education is the key to transforming lives and to guaranteeing the future in our American democracy.

- Fourth, I hope you will be able, as a result of reading *The Quiet Crisis*, to stand back, look at the big picture, see through the big picture to the future, and begin to make your own action plan for how the future should look.

Peter Smith
August 2003

Introduction

American higher education is a wonder of the modern world. Stretching from the tip of Machias, Maine, to the Big Island in Hawaii, and from Key West to Nome, it is without parallel in human history.

I work at California State University (CSU), the largest university in America. It serves a state so economically large and diverse that were California an independent nation, its gross national product would be the fifth largest in the world. The university itself educates more students in a year than attended all American colleges and universities in 1900—now more than 400,000 full- and part-time students every year.

Not only is American higher education expansive, it is diverse. This nation hosts more than 4,000 colleges ranging from two-year to doctoral, public, private, liberal arts, and technical institutes, religious and nonsectarian (U.S. Department of Education, 2001). The list is long and the variety is amazing.

Furthermore, if you look closely at this wonder of wonders, you will be reminded that our system of higher education is not a system at all. Some institutions are affiliated with others; some are not. Some have storied histories and global alumni groups; others' names are barely known within their own neighborhoods. Although each is considered a postsecondary institution, each has its unique history, mission, and orientation. They are a set of highly autonomous, independent institutions, vigorously resistant to any over arching or outside control. In fact, Americans do not want their colleges and universities to be all the same or do all the same things. This independence of thought and action is as American as apple pie.

Americans delight in the differences among colleges and universities in part because we delight in our variety as people. Some children want to be brain surgeons; others long to be teachers. As a society, we value both professions; thus, by extension, we value the different training that each requires. Given the wide range of interests and occupations that sustain our communities, it only makes sense that there be an equally diverse set of higher education options available to us. So we've achieved a sort of national consensus around the idea that colleges of great value to the individual learner may also be very different from each other.

Despite this diversity of mission, orientation, and governance, however, the operating structure and assumptions behind how colleges and universities do their business have changed less over the last 300 years than any other Western institution. In fact, when Vatican II lifted Latin from the Roman Catholic mass, this observation probably became true. Virtually all of our schools, from nursery schools to post-graduate institutes, reflect an educational model that has been in place since the 14th century. This operational model is based on assumptions and traditions that have long outlived not only their usefulness but also their logic. For example, the idea of a scholar-professor standing in front of students to speak in a lecture format predates the printing press. Our academic calendars are perfectly matched to the needs of an agricultural society now long dead. Although our society needs graduates who are educated to critically consider and apply knowledge in the outside world, most education occurs in a traditional academic environment. And we still operate on the assumption that all important teaching and learning happens in school classrooms, regardless of their type. All too often, the connection between a typical university curriculum and the actual, lived experiences of today's university students is largely nonexistent.

To put it another way, although we have opened the doors of opportunity, we have not changed the teaching model. I am not writing about something slightly outmoded, as if we've drawn a fundamental concept from pre-fax days or the "dark age" my children experienced before the advent of MTV. I am speaking of the basic academic model of American education with a teacher in front of a class of students. Americans have inherited, without significant modification, a system of education that is as outdated, outmoded, and outlandish as an ox cart plodding down Interstate 405.

Within our diversity of institutional form and behind our historic commitment to access, there is a numbing sameness within our institutions when it comes to teaching and learning. The heart of the quiet crisis enveloping America's colleges lies where we actually do higher education, in our classrooms and traditions.

Different colleges recruit different students, serve different audiences, and teach different knowledge, but they do it through the same basic model: with a scholar-professor in front of students, isolated from the world, organized into standard blocks of time with a central text or syllabus that will fill a three-credit course with papers, exams, and grades. The sameness of how we teach from one campus to another is staggering. We are universal in expecting the same thing from our students: to come as they are and be ready to learn, to absorb the teaching, prove they learned it, and go on to a higher level for more of the same. Accounting and history, chemistry and psychology are presented the same way. The wealthiest, most elite university in the East subjects its students to largely the same process that will be suffered by the newest recruit at a community college in New Mexico. And while technology has certainly modified many a course structure, the reality is that the course design continues to treat all students largely the same when it comes to teaching, and the cost of technology is treated as an add-on, not an investment in transformation.

This sameness would have as a parallel hundreds of restaurants, each claiming to be unique, all serving one dish: white rice. Some might be fried, some might be steamed with saffron. Some might even be part of a fricassee dish. But it's all rice. No matter where you go, which campus you visit, what students you interview, the assumptions behind teaching and learning are unchanged. At Yale and Yakima, backpack-wearing students absorb knowledge from someone wiser, regurgitate that knowledge to the wiser person's satisfaction, receive grades, and move on to sit in more classes, absorb knowledge from someone wiser, and so on.

This classic academic model has worked pretty well for America over the last 250 years, so what is the problem? The problem is that continuing to rely on it flies directly in the face of what we know about how people learn, the opportunities that technology presents to transform the educational enterprise, and our historic record of failure with a rapidly diversifying population. The traditional academic model won't harness and integrate the extraordinary technological resources we are creating that have the capacity to transform teaching and learning. And it won't make room for the new knowledge being created about the many ways that intelligence works and people learn. In plain terms, it won't get us where we want to go as a society committed to equal opportunity for all.

The consequences of the crisis surrounding American higher education will not be quiet much longer. Business leaders cry in vain for higher education that equips employees to compete in a global marketplace. Community leaders watch school taxes (or local college tuitions) rise while voter participation falls and graduation rates stagnate. And parents continue to watch children who are sunny and bright at home become quiet and unsuccessful in school. The learning gap between rich and poor, Hispanic and black and white, urban and suburban, children of immigrants and children of pilgrim descendents is growing. And ever-larger percentages of poor and ethnically diverse children swell our elementary and high schools.

In fact, the news that our educational systems are failing isn't news at all; it is headlined, accepted truth. What's kept out of the headlines is the fundamental cause of this failure. We have blamed the students, their parents, the society, the teachers, and other associated culprits who have been seen near the scene of the crime. But, in fact, schools do not work in the 21st century because they are organized around assumptions based in 14th century Europe. And as the makeup of our learners diversifies, as American society becomes evermore digital and wired, as we are asked to become more successful with more learners, the consequences of relying on outdated assumptions and models become downright dangerous.

What do we want from higher education? Recall with me the opening scene of the movie classic *Animal House*. A character played by the late John Belushi, surrounded by collegiate cohorts, is lounging at the base of a statue on his college's campus. Below the sculpture appears the inscription "Knowledge Is Good." The audience, seeing hung-over students beneath the lofty inscription, is immediately laughing. The contradiction of college characters and college aspirations is blatant. This campus is, obviously, a soporific place where little is taught and less is learned. The remainder of the movie is a madcap satiric comedy that pierces the veil of academic pomposity with a zany caricature of the college experience. No one comes off well: not students, not faculty, not administration.

Like any good satire, *Animal House* is uproariously funny. Remembering that those who wrote the screenplay were graduates of Harvard and veterans of the *National Lampoon*, drawing laughs at the expense of the nation's most elite universities, the movie's spoofs are exquisite. But in the end, the story provokes a disquieting question: In fact, what do we want from our colleges and universities? Most parents, students, educators, and policy writers would easily confess, "I don't know, but this isn't it!" I suppose that's helpful, but not very. Knowing what we don't want merely confirms the question. We need a much better answer.

Americans want a lot from higher education. Along with the diversity of colleges and universities, most Americans also agree that all the people who meet basic entrance requirements and have shown some capacity to succeed should have access to a college education. We believe that for every capable student there must be an available, effective source of higher education. Policymakers want accountable institutions that educate broadly and create a competitive workforce at a reasonable price. Parents want a safe place for their children to learn, enter adulthood, get a degree, and get a good job. Younger students want to be released from parental bondage and set free to be with others who share their tastes and beliefs. Older students want efficiency and cost-effectiveness, a quick turnaround on their degree and convenient schedules accommodating work and family demands. Employers need graduates who can think critically, work in teams, solve problems, write and speak clearly, and work across cultural lines in a global society. Recent immigrants and their children, or members of populations long dispossessed, want a seat at the table of opportunity. And millions of Americans want their favorite source of higher education to produce outstanding football champions and basketball powerhouses.

Not surprisingly, this chaos of expectations has increasingly fueled America's love-hate relationship with higher education at all levels. We love our colleges and universities when we think of cutting-edge, lifesaving research; when we think of the opportunity an education offers, the value of a college degree in the marketplace, and the prestige that comes with graduation; and when we hear marching bands on a warm fall afternoon or stories of graduates who've gone on to change the course of history.

But these same colleges and universities can also be baffling, distant, insensitive bureaucracies when the curriculum or the teaching style of a particular professor just doesn't meet a student's needs. They are, too often, not learner-friendly, but frustratingly unresponsive to individual needs, and islands isolated from the crises and woes of their own communities. For first-generation college students coming from cultural backgrounds that lie outside of the economic and social mainstream of America, this adds a potentially crushing burden to the already heavy load of going to college.

Colleges may offer an extraordinary array of courses. But when those courses aren't available this year or the professors' "my way or the highway" attitude silences some students and drives others out the door, feelings of affection can change to anger and betrayal. We love our institutions of higher education for their promise and their potential. But we are far more skeptical of their ability to actually deliver.

Watch a business channel on cable television, and you'll have an opportunity to see America's businesses broadcasting their annual meetings. Speakers are in casual clothing; their presentations are marked by high-tech, fast-moving video; they engage their audience with immediate-response devices. This is the corporate ritual, thoroughly and absolutely fixed on today's capabilities and tomorrow's opportunities. Nothing about it is outdated or outmoded.

Now think of a course catalog at any college: thick, filled with offerings that are not always available, sometimes online, often not. New students are left to dig out the valuable information, often on their own. "What should I take? When can I get it? Who can help me?" they ask. And always, the same basic teaching model.

Compare the corporate meeting with the course catalog and ask yourself, "Which of these institutions appears ready to make a difference in today's world?"

It is honorable that the roots of any institution are planted deep in tradition. But all too often our colleges and universities treasure tradition at the expense of today's knowledge, research, and needs. We practice an outdated model of education. Its effectiveness is limited. And it's time for a change.

Students come to college wanting at least one thing: personal change. Colleges and universities promise to change students' lives through education. This promise is as bold as it is unique to the American offer of opportunity. We say, "Spend your time with us, learn with us. When we are finished with your academic journey, you will be a different person, and your life will be on a different trajectory because of the experience."

We want colleges to change students' lives through learning. Pity the person who, heading for her first day of college, assures her family, "I'll be back in four or five years and I'll be just the same." Older students who work and attend college in the evening do it to change. All learning is about change. In American mythology, colleges are the gateway to opportunity, leading to better lives, better jobs, more power, and more money. And the myth of the gateway is built on change, personal change, for learners through education. But too often, the individual doesn't appear to matter to our colleges and universities.

It is no wonder that some business and political leaders, looking at universities and their habits and traditions, conclude that the world of higher education is out of step with the needs of a global economy.

Like us, at times they cheer our colleges and universities. At other times, they shake their heads and occasionally their fists.

The good news is that almost everyone believes in the importance of higher education. Few critics suggest that the system be dismantled, that it has outlived its usefulness. Almost to a person they want to improve it, make it more responsive to the needs of learners and the society. Over the past 35 years a four-year, baccalaureate degree has become the main portal to the American dream. In 1980, the earnings gap between those with a college degree versus those without was 50%; today, it's closer to 100% (Mishel, Bernstein, & Schmidt, 2001). With a college degree and the skills and intellectual characteristics that it represents, you have a chance. Without them, you probably don't. We all know that a college education is more important than ever.

But the bad news is that there is growing doubt that higher education, in its traditional form, can meet the needs facing America. Societal institutions prosper because they do something that the society at large cannot do better on its own. Put another way, effective institutions make goods and services available to their community, or market, that would otherwise not be available on equal or better terms. As long as they are useful, they survive. Universities, like all other institutions, are governed by this law.

Colleges and universities are faced with a new dilemma. We have succeeded in creating enormous opportunity through financial and physical access to college. We've vastly increased access to the scholar professor on modern campuses. We've opened doors of opportunity that were closed in the past. But once learners are through the front door, the pathway to success is tortured. Students and their learning are not the organizing center; faculty and tradition are. Knowledge is not based on community-defined need; it is contained in this year's version of last year's syllabus. Faculty teaching loads, schedules, gaining tenure, and attracting research funding take priority over student learning. And technology is seen, all too often, as an add-on.

The myth that the current structure of schools and the historic assumptions about education are the best way to educate people in the 21st century still dominates parents and policymakers from local school boards to colleges and universities to the Congress of the United States. If professional educators whisper that "how we teach doesn't encourage learning," they are viewed by peers and colleagues as either naïve idealists or trouble-seeking heretics. If thoughtful policymakers offer proposals to reform learning by re-purposing schools, they are dismissed as a serious force. Teachers' unions, often whipping boys for conservatives, defend the current model because it is the model that justifies teachers' unions. But staunch conservatives defend the current model, or an even older, throwback model ("Back to the Basics" with McGuffey's Reader) because it is the model that parallels their philosophy. So, like a family with a drunken uncle upstairs and out of sight, we debate the situation. But the status quo is very powerful, so the situation persists.

This crisis belongs to all of us. It belongs to the policymakers in Washington, D.C., where higher education is at the forefront of everyone's attention. We need more than we achieved during the days when I was a congressman. The federal policy of the 21st century cannot simply react to the needs generated by past practice. It must be bold, anticipating the impending needs of a dynamic and rapidly changing society, and preparing the way for a radically different education delivery system than the one we currently have.

This crisis also belongs to any American who genuinely cares about equality and justice in this nation. The average wage disparity in the United States between those with a bachelor's degree and those who completed high school has now reached almost 100%, or $1,000,000 over a lifetime. Because this disparity falls along lines of race, economics, and social status, our education systems are contributing to perpetuating two societies in America.

And those of us who are educators and policymakers need to own the crisis as our own. We know how learning occurs, and how it does not occur. When we perpetuate an academic model and institutional forms that allow only a narrow definition of how learning occurs, we are failing, not only ourselves but also our students, our communities, and our nation. We owe America genuine learning that is responsive to the needs, the knowledge, and the potential of the 21st century.

The Quiet Crisis is a critique and a policy primer for higher education administrators, policymakers, parents, students, and other people interested in reshaping and extending American higher education so that it more effectively serves the needs of the emerging population. It calls for universities and colleges to move beyond incremental and adaptive change to new organizational forms that are as reflective of the society around them as the early lecture was to the lack of books. I've been involved with American colleges as a student, professor, and president and as a parent, policymaker, and politician for my entire adult life. I am as responsible as anyone for the silence that has filled this arena. And I hope to take some responsibility for ending it.

PART ONE
THE QUIET CRISIS

1

▼

THE OPPORTUNITY PROMISE

Even-numbered years bring with them a distinctively American tradition. Every two years in the U.S. Congress, every four years in the American presidency, and every six years in the U.S. Senate, incumbents are sent out to face the electorate who are invited to thank them with their votes or throw the rascals out. Generally, we do a little of both. Sometimes election results are the consequence of the individual in question, our affinity with them, or our distaste for what they've done. But sometimes incumbents are simply trapped in a swirling national mood that either blesses the status quo or demands change. We've achieved a national stability in our political system that has seldom, if ever, been found elsewhere. We have stability despite constant change, in spite of brawling candidates, competing parties, and shifting national agendas.

I arrived at the U.S. Congress in 1989. With other first-time members, I showed up full of newly minted hope and the optimism that marks people who've won. After all, an electorate had told each of us that we were trusted to deliver to them, and to the nation, all that America had promised. If we were, as most freshman classes are, a bit presumptuous and a little too impressed with ourselves, we were also sincere. We intended not simply to tend the fires of democracy but also to stoke them.

It may not have been until I felt the sting of losing an election, and experienced the changeover in office from the perspective of the one who's leaving, that I fully appreciated the power of the American system of democracy. Perhaps then, more than ever before, I recognized that the answer to the question "What's unique about American democracy?" is this: We endure, as a democracy, because we have the means to change.

I was raised as a child in an age when the word "permanence" was applied to whatever resisted change, whatever did not change and could not be changed. The pillars in front of the local bank. The Latin of the priest's mass. The smell of hallways in every school. I lived a Norman Rockwell childhood. In that time and place, to be permanent was to be unmovable, unalterable.

Then I learned of the hairy mastodon, that brutish beast, half-elephant and half-buffalo, whose life ended when temperatures plummeted into an Ice Age. The body of a mastodon was recovered from deep in some arctic grave, its stomach still full of fresh green grass. It had probably been wondering where it might find dinner in the evening when the Ice Age captured it. The hoary beast did not live because it could not change fast enough.

Change: The Lifeblood of Permanency

Considering the mastodon, I reconsidered "permanence." Change is not the enemy of permanence; it is its lifeblood. Food co-ops challenge supermarkets. The financial corporation that bought our village bank soon leveled the building; the pillars were dust to dust. But the bank is still open because, in its larger version, it is able to compete and survive. And credit unions are available for people who prefer the more personal, local touch. Latin is gone not only from high schools but also most masses, but the ancient faith contained in the mass still infuses the Roman Catholic tradition. Only the smell of the opening day of school has endured, and, in this innocent fact lies a harbinger of some danger. Our systems of education seem to have been the most risk-averse, the most effective at resisting and avoiding necessary change.

The core characteristic of American democracy—the feature that gives it enduring vitality—is the broadly understood commitment to renew our structures of government, whenever necessary, to better serve the people represented by that government. We have ways to assure change that will enable us to have permanence. We do not need to revolt; we can reform.

This is no modern discovery. The founding fathers struggled to agree on a delicate balance between the need for stability in the present and the need for change over time. They knew instinctively that without stability there would be no order. But they also understood that change was the means of survival, the only route to lasting national prosperity. It's a testimony to their genius that long before we discussed global change in conversations bounced off satellites, they inserted provisions into the Constitution allowing the institutions they were creating in a horse-and-buggy age to adapt to the changing needs of an unimagined future.

If you visit the Jefferson Memorial in Washington, D.C., and read his wisdom, carved into a wall, you will see that he compares the first Constitution to a set of children's clothes. Jefferson and his colleagues knew the shape of government would need to be recut and restyled as the country grew. "I am not an advocate for frequent changes in laws and constitution," he wrote, "but laws and institutions go hand in hand with the progress of the human mind . . . We might as well require a man to wear the same coat that fitted him when he was a boy . . . [as ask the original version of the constitution to serve the future needs of the country without amendment]."

This ability to achieve fundamental change while maintaining essential stability of government and society is what brings renewal and reinvigoration to our democracy. Over time, our American democracy breathes, inhaling new ideas and exhaling old practices and paradigms. The Constitution, the Bill of Rights, the separation of powers—they are sometimes seen as the pillars of our democracy, unchanged and unchanging. But that's not true. They are less like rigid pillars, permanent in my childhood sense, than they are like sturdy scaffolding, the stuff we disassemble and reassemble so we can stand in the right place to continually build and rebuild the democracy.

What's really permanent, what truly endures, is the soul of our democracy. And deep in America's soul lies the promise of opportunity, of liberty and freedom for every person, the opportunity to create a better future for our children than the one we inherited from our parents. We are committed, everywhere, to the basic promise of opportunity for each person. With this commitment, we will survive. Without it, we will decline. And, if the promise of opportunity lies in the soul of America's continuing social and political revolution, then education and learning—the lifeblood of opportunity—is at the heart of this promise in the 21st century. Education is the path to the table of opportunity in 21st-century America.

The Promise of Education
Education has been a promise in America since our earliest days as a republic. Our founding fathers and mothers were committed to learning. The fledgling government took its first step toward the education of its citizens in 1787 when Congress passed a law requiring states in the Northwest Territory to set aside a plot of land in each township for common schools.

Seventy-five years later in 1862, as war clouds gathered, Congress passed the Morrill Act, establishing colleges of agriculture and scientific studies. Sponsored by Senator Justin Morrill of Vermont, the act was the first major federal activity in education. If, for example, you walk the campus of Michigan State University, you are strolling across history and between buildings that owe their existence to the Morrill Act. Just five years later another bold step was taken. While titled "An Act to Establish a Department of Education," the 1867 law's primary purpose was to "collect such statistics and facts as shall show the condition and progress of education in the several States and Territories."

Behind this early legislation stood the pioneer conviction that education and learning are keys to the American dream. During the half-century that followed these acts, America became a nation of immigrants chasing the dream from the rich soils of Iowa to the booming gold fields of California. What brought the immigrants was the belief that opportunity awaited them in America.

Learning Without the Promise
The connection between education and opportunity that I've described here as history and values is, in fact, deeply and painfully rooted in

my own experience. In 1971, at an early spring meeting in the 4-C Center in Barton, Vermont, a woman named Margery Moore delivered a stunning message to me.

A small group of us were starting a new college, the Community College of Vermont. The meeting in question was one of many community informational sessions we were holding to sell our idea to potential students across the region. In most of these gatherings, we'd preached and others had listened. But Marjorie changed that, and us.

Our college was designed to serve people who for reasons of geography, income, or prior education could not go to college. Vermont in 1971 was too small, too poor, and too rural to support a traditional campus and faculty. Just as the electric cooperative movement of the 1930s took electricity where the corporations wouldn't, giving hill farmers a chance to employ modern methods even at the end of Vermont's dirt roads, we decided to take education to the learners. We designed a noncampus college built around what Vermont did have: people, programs, need, and community spirit. We used qualified community people to teach, and existing facilities—high schools, churches, homes, and businesses—as learning sites. We developed an outcomes-based curriculum to assure quality in each setting—proof that the identified needs of people in each community were being met.

There was just one problem. As a new institution, it would be much easier if we could offer the learning without academic credit. So we proposed a rich menu of learning opportunities, available locally, anytime—but no academic credit. This would be learning for its own intrinsic value, so that learners could improve their lot in life.

Margery Moore would have none of it. A woman with commanding presence, she loomed in the back of the hall and roared, "You, with your degrees from Princeton and Harvard, you're telling us that we don't need credit, we don't need degrees? When you live your life without a degree, then I'll think about it. But you never will." She was putting the ax to our sacred tree. We were awestruck.

Then she personalized it. "Peter," she said, her voice full of Vermont wisdom, "if it's good enough for you, it's good enough for us."

I was 25 years old, full of enthusiasm, an idealist. Margery Moore was hardened by her life, more practical. I knew, intuitively, that she was right. Her righteous anger burned at me all the way home that night because she had truth on her side. Our model was no more than half a loaf: We were offering education, but not opportunity. We were promising the thrill of learning but withholding the power it could bring, the power that attached to credits, diplomas, and a resume that fetches a job or a raise. Painfully, I recognized the noblesse oblige in what we were proposing. We had worshipped abstract ideals; Margery had tempered our ideals with hard reality. What she wanted, what she demanded—and, I soon acknowledged, what she had been promised in America—was learning as a strategy to achieve opportunity. We had not thought about that. But we began to. It made the task of developing a college far more complicated. But Margery Moore's better wisdom redeemed us from our own potential failure.

A Seat at the Table of Opportunity

Somewhere in the quiet beauty of that Vermont winter I began to see that, although I was no longer a graduate student, my learning had not only continued, it was accelerating. Margery Moore, with her high school diploma, had been a potent teacher. She reminded me, indeed she taught me, that education is the promised instrument of opportunity in America. When our college, with all its innovative policies and features, was accredited; when people like Margery Moore could emerge not only with learning but also with degrees to seize the opportunity it granted; then I could say we were keeping the American vision of a nation with unlimited seats at the table of opportunity.

The promise of opportunity for all in an increasingly diverse America is more important than ever. Without opportunity, the number of seats at the table of opportunity will be limited for the few. And people will get to it by waiting in line, knocking others off their chairs, or seizing a space with force. This is a description of aristocracy, not America. Completing a postsecondary education is the ticket to a seat at the table of opportunity. Today, our prisons are bursting at the seams, populated largely with poor men, many of color, who failed to even graduate from high school. We know the penalties for educational failure are stiff and mean, and the costs to society are enormous.

Raul Yzaguirre, president of La Raza, the United States' largest Hispanic organization, spoke to a gathering on Capitol Hill late in 2001. His gentle voice filled with conviction when he said, "The education gap between the Hispanic and majority community is not narrowing, it's getting wider. And at the same time, especially for you members of Congress, I need to remind you that the American public school system, when it comes to Hispanics, isn't a pipeline; it's a sieve."

He is right, and for more learners than just Hispanics. We have a proud tradition of increasing access for all. Like an aging artery, however, the pipeline to college has major blockages, and the fresh blood is not getting through to our heart.

Since the G.I. Bill's passage in June 1944, we have built a means of access for higher education—a way of getting into college—second to none in human history. Four years after the close of World War II (1949) there were 1,851 degree-granting institutions in America. Today, there are over 4,000. They come in every shape, size, and type, from seminaries to trade schools, from the state universities of the Midwest to Ivy League research centers and football powerhouses.

Those who lived through these years witnessed the phenomenal rise of community colleges and the concurrent expansion of state colleges and universities. We've more than doubled the number of colleges by legislating dollars at both the federal and state levels, pouring public funds into coffers also holding private contributions, and student payments. We have done this because we hold one, collective goal: an affordable, high-quality college education within easy reach of each American.

In some important respects, we've succeeded beyond our fathers' and mothers' wildest dreams. Immediately after World War II, 30% of the relevant age cohort enrolled in higher education in the United States. For a comparison, look to the Europe of that time where an elite higher education system was maintained with fewer than 5% of citizens attending postsecondary institutions. By 1960, Europe had increased access to more than 15% of the student-age population while the United States was approaching 50% of possible students actually seeking entry to college.

In the half-century since that time, however—through days of the civil rights movement, the rise of feminism, the advances into technology and space, the shrinking world and growing global economy—our strides toward achieving the American promise of opportunity in higher education have shrunk. Although it is true we are graduating more students than ever, our success rates are flattening as a percentage of the total population. We are winnowing out the very people we need if we, as a nation, want to compete in a global market.

We are leaving behind millions of Americans who have the capacity to learn and for whom the promise of opportunity was made but not kept.

How We Have Failed

Our relative failure lies in those parts of the population that are growing fastest. When asked to succeed with an ever-changing and expanding population of learners, diverse in their cultural experiences and educational preparation as well as their approaches to learning, our institutions gasp and struggle. The gasping is becoming more labored. We have increased undergraduate minority student enrollments, but we have not fundamentally changed either the culture or the pedagogy— the means of learning—that should have accompanied this shift.

As a result, the struggle is not producing the results we need. While minority students represented 17% of the undergraduate students in 1976, they increased to 27% of the student body by 1999. That's the good news. The bad news is that 28% of white students completed a bachelor's degree in 2000, compared with less than 17% of African-Americans and 11% of Hispanics (Burn, 2002). Stated simply, none of our nation's students, especially minority students, are achieving college degrees at rates commensurate with their capacity and at levels acceptable for society's long-term well-being. When one combines the population increases for minorities with the disparity in college achievement, we are risking a nation split by the educational and occupational gaps rising from this disparity. Unless we can apply appropriate models of education for all these groups, we will never deliver the promise that holds America together—opportunity that rises from learning.

In stark contrast to this failure to thrive among low-income students, first-generation college goers, and students of color, Americans' expectations about education have continued to increase. The right to an education—a dream from 1850 to 1900, a hope from 1900 to 1950, and a goal from 1950 to 2000—is now an expectation across our society. And the economic benefits are clear. We have promised America a table with enough chairs for every child. And 35 million Hispanic-Americans, among others, are willing to work for the American promise of opportunity. Our national integrity demands that we never apportion opportunity, let alone on the basis of class, race, belief, or gender. Yet, de facto, as we hide behind our structures, models, and traditions and struggle with budgets that won't fund our maturing and exclusive institutional structures, that is exactly what we are doing.

Affirming the promise is nice rhetoric; keeping it is critical to the future of our country and the promise of representative democracy. America is becoming a two-class society, and the great divide between the classes is education. College graduates earn almost 100% more than high school graduates in their lives. In 1970, no fewer than 8,581,000 citizens were enrolled in college. Projections for 2007 suggest that 15,929,000 citizens will be enrolled in higher education, a doubling in the number of college students over a 30-year span. More people going to college is good news. It also means, however, that, for every opening in the American job market, the likelihood that a college graduate will be one of the competitors has vastly increased. So, regardless of what else happens, we know that the skill and knowledge requirements for employment and the jobs requiring those skills are both increasing. Therefore, for every noncollege graduate, good options in the job market, as defined by status, income, opportunity for promotion, will become constantly more elusive and dependent on having a higher education.

It's time to deliver on the opportunity promise. If you look at our record of success beginning in the ninth grade, our record for successfully graduating learners from college tells the story of Raul Yzaguirre's sieve. We know the old saw, "Lies, damn lies, and statistics."

But at the policy level, our record tells a painful truth (see Figure 1.1). Nationally, in 2000, on average only two-thirds of our ninth-graders graduated from high school, with 38% continuing to college. Six years later, only 18% of those ninth-graders have graduated from college. From 100% in the ninth grade to 18% graduating within 10 years. Furthermore, several studies show huge discrepancies by race and income in the transition from high school to college with less than 30% of Hispanics, 50% of blacks, and 60% of whites successfully making the leap from the ninth grade to college.

Focus for a moment not simply on the totals but on the gaps between white, black, and Hispanic students. Our newer, poorer, and historically dispossessed and first-generation student populations are increasing at a faster rate than our success ratios with them. In the next 12 to 15 years, we will witness a growth in the nation's traditional undergraduate population of at least 2.6 million students. Of these, 2 million will be people of color (Swail, 2002). When you see these gaps over time, repeated year after year, they point the way to an educational and economic aristocracy taking the place of an American promise. First, students graduate from high school in disproportionate racial groupings; that's troubling enough. But, second, even for those who do graduate from high school, the probability of going to college and graduating is less for those who are poor and ethnic minorities. This gap suggests an inevitable decline for them and our society. When you consider that our future population growth will be heavily in the populations who are not succeeding in school, you can see that we are looking disaster in the face.

And there's a lot more talent and intelligence out there than our schools are picking up. Consider the case of Bob DePrato:

When I was 18, I joined the Army. That was when I got plugged into the world because, before that, it was just Jersey City. I didn't know any other cultures or customs or what people perceived as normal.

I went into the Army just before Vietnam got hot. Kennedy had just signed a bill giving married people a lower draft priority, so I had all these guys with college deferments coming in. As they graduated from college, they were getting picked off and they were coming because, although there was a war at the time, it was still a volunteer war.

I was a loser, a high school dropout, and I wound up in a platoon with college graduates at a survey school. To this day, I believe it was a screw up. I got assigned to a school that required higher mathematics—you had to know trig functions—and I hadn't even taken high school algebra.

Guys there had graduated from every college in the country, from San Jose State to Cornell, the cream of United States education. Two hundred men. Ninety-nine percent of them got drafted after their deferments were up. They were really sharp guys, but they were just poking through.

I got a lot from these guys. They took me around. They were a more elite crowd. At that time I didn't know anybody that played bridge or golf to begin with. These guys didn't slight me. They weren't crass. They were nice people and they said, "You look like a pretty sharp kid." I said, "What do you mean, a sharp kid? I dropped out of high school when I was seventeen years old. "They all said, "You can change that."

When you're programmed to be a loser for seventeen years, you don't stop being a loser just because somebody says you're not a loser. It doesn't work that way. You think about it and you say, "Hey, I hope he's right," but you just don't know what to do. We were together maybe ninety days or six months, then we were sent to the four corners of the earth. They definitely left me with something, though I still had a confidence problem.

Something else happened to me in the Army. I picked up my high school equivalency. It was five hours out of the day and it plugged me into so many jobs. I often think about that. Five hours. You sit down and fill in a whole bunch of IBM holes and it turns your life around. I wouldn't be here today if I didn't have those five hours. I'd still be saying, "I can't be this because I don't know how to do algebra." That's a big problem. People cancel themselves out before they even inquire. (Smith, 1986, pp. 50–51)

A small group of men and the United States Army taught a nobody what America's educational system has failed to teach millions: They are, each of them, a somebody. They are learners, becoming equipped for work and service to their community.

Figure 1.1
Student Pipeline: Transition and Completion Rates
From Ninth Grade to College

	Percentage of ninth-graders who graduate from high school on time, go directly to college, return for their second year, and graduate within 150% of program time	For every 100 ninth-graders	# graduate from high school	# enter college	# are still enrolled their sophomore year	# graduate within 150% time	Percent of population 25–44 with a bachelor's degree or higher in 2000
Alabama	13	100	58.9	34	23	13	21
Alaska	6	100	62.3	28		6	22
Arizona	14	100	59.3	30	18	14	23
Arkansas	12	100	73.6	39	26	12	18
California	17	100	68.7	33	22	17	27
Colorado	18	100	70.5	37	26	18	34
Connecticut	26	100	77	48	37	26	35
Delaware	19	100	60.7	36	28	19	28
Florida	14	100	55.2	32	23	14	24
Georgia	12	100	52.3	32	21	12	27
Hawaii	13	100	64.2	38	22	13	27
Idaho	14	100	76.9	34	23	14	22
Illinois	19	100	71.1	43	29	19	30
Indiana	21	100	68.2	41	30	21	22
Iowa	28	100	83	54	37	28	25
Kansas	22	100	74.4	50	32	22	29
Kentucky	13	100	65.8	39	25	13	19
Louisiana	12	100	56.2	33	22	12	20
Maine	23	100	76.6	42	31	23	23
Maryland	18	100	73.3	40	30	18	34
Massachusetts	28	100	74.8	52	41	28	39

Michigan	18	100	68.7	40	28	18	24
Minnesota	25	100	83.7	53	38	25	32
Mississippi	13	100	56	36	23	13	18
Missouri	18	100	73	39	27	18	25
Montana	17	100	78.1	42	28	17	25
Nebraska	22	100	83.8	50	38	22	28
Nevada	11	100	68.8	28	19	11	18
New Hampshire	27	100	73.9	44	34	27	30
New Jersey	24	100	86.1	55	40	24	34
New Mexico	11	100	60.3	36	22	11	21
New York	18	100	58.6	37	28	18	31
North Carolina	18	100	58.7	38	28	18	25
North Dakota	24	100	84.1	58	42	24	26
Ohio	17	100	69.6	39	28	17	24
Oklahoma	12	100	72.8	36	23	12	21
Oregon	15	100	67.4	34	23	15	26
Pennsylvania	27	100	74.9	46	36	27	27
Rhode Island	26	100	69.5	46	37	26	29
South Carolina	14	100	51	34	23	14	22
South Dakota	22	100	74.2	47	31	22	25
Tennessee	14	100	54.8	34	23	14	22
Texas	11	100	61.9	32	19	11	24
Utah	16	100	83.9	32	21	16	26
Vermont	21	100	78.7	36	28	21	30
Virginia	20	100	73.9	39	30	20	32
Washington	16	100	70.8	32	22	16	28
West Virginia	15	100	74.8	39	27	15	17
Wisconsin	22	100	78	45	33	22	25
Wyoming	18	100	75	39		18	22
Nation	18	100	67.1	38	26	18	27

Source: Mortenson, T. (2002). ACT institutional survey, NCES–IPEDS graduation rate survey. Boulder, CO: The National Center for Higher Education Management Systems. Retrieved December 16, 2003, from http://www.higheredinfo.org/dbrowser/index.php?submeasure=119&year=2000&level=nation&mode=data&state=0

For the last 75 years, we've asked Americans to believe that the promise of opportunity is for all who would share it, not the few who began with it. Our children can surpass us. We've repeatedly reaffirmed this commitment. Now the demand for delivering what we've promised has passed the point of no return as a tidal wave of ethnic and economic diversity pushes people toward the table of opportunity. No longer is the promise of opportunity a covenant for the few. Now it must be a guarantee for the many, including those dispossessed throughout our nation's history for all the myriad reasons. Those knocking on the door of our colleges and universities—if they dare knock at all—are increasingly people of color, people of working-class poverty, and people whose parents have actually believed the promise we made.

So, what is our record in terms of finishing the job? Let me repeat: For the year 2000 the National Center for Higher Education Management Systems (NCHEMS) reports that out of 100 ninth-graders, 18 graduated within 10 years with either a BA or an AA (see Figure 1.1)! In California, more than 30% of those who enter ninth grade do not graduate. Far above the previously reported record of 12%. Now that's a sieve!

Conclusion: Improving the Completion Rates for All Students
The challenge facing American higher education is not simply to improve access, but also to dramatically improve the completion rates for these students with whom we have not been historically successful. And we can't improve our completion rate without diversifying and rethinking the way we do business. Let's be clear. The problem is greater than whether we are successful with the majority of students that we currently see. We must learn how to succeed with millions of additional students whom we don't currently see, from populations that we have historically failed. And that will take the rethinking and repurposing of colleges and universities.

There remains today one common academic model for the delivery of postsecondary education around the world. At the center of the institution stands the professor who is enshrined with the autonomy essential to academic freedom. This model assumes the direct transfer of learning from one person who knows to another person who does not (Altbach, Berdahl, & Gumport, 1998). It is a model as outdated as the ox cart. It does not recognize new community concerns, new student needs, new economic realities, new technological options and new demands for skilled workers. It reveals colleges and universities as moribund institutions that are not, despite their names, learning organizations. To assure our permanence and keep the opportunity promise, we must learn how to change.

2

▼

Universities as Learning Organizations

Peter Senge is a teacher whose name is known in every major corporate headquarters in America. His landmark book *The Fifth Discipline: The Art & Practice of The Learning Organization* (1990) changed both our vocabulary and our way of thinking. Senge taught leaders that if they wanted the organization they led—an army, a factory, a temple, a TV network—to endure, to have permanence, they would need to give it what America's founding fathers had given the nation: a way to change.

In brief, what Senge said was that the primary strategy for change is learning. Everything around your organization is changing: your markets, your customers, your labor pools, your competitor's products and advertising strategies. You must compete with global organizations based on one continent, funded on another, importing products from yet a third. The only way to survive in this constantly changing context, said Senge, is to learn more than others do, faster than they do. If you are best at learning you'll adjust to the new contexts first, spotting real opportunities and avoiding threats while achieving your objectives. Learning is key to change. It is such an obvious truth that many of us had missed it.

Most people's eyes glaze over if you talk to them about "learning" or "learning organizations." Little wonder—for, in everyday use, learning has come to be synonymous with "taking in information." Yet, taking in information is only distantly related to real learning. It would be nonsensical to say, "I just read a great book about bicycle riding—I've now learned that." Real learning gets to the heart of what it means to be human. Through learning we re-create ourselves. Through learning we become able to do something we never were able to do. Through learning we re-perceive the world and our relationship to it. Through learning we extend our capacity to create, to be part of the generative process of life. There is within each of us a deep hunger for this type of learning. (Senge, 1999, pp. 13–14)

Senge showed us all that given the constantly shifting global economies and cultures within which we now live, only those organizations that learn quickly and wisely will adapt quickly and wisely. Without such adaptation or change, organizations will not survive. They will be mastodons trapped under the ice of history.

What's more, Senge believes—as do I—that such learning is not only possible. It's natural.

Learning organizations are possible because, deep down, we are all learners. No one has to teach an infant to learn. In fact, no one has to teach infants anything. They are intrinsically inquisitive, masterful learners who learn to walk, speak, and pretty much run their households all on their own. Learning organizations are possible because not only is it our nature to learn but we love to learn. (Senge, 1990, p. 4)

Senge is right. Human beings are born learners. Learning is as natural to children as breathing. But when most children enter school they find an institution that's dedicated to teaching, not to learning as Senge describes it. The institution of the school was invented in another time and place, built on a set of assumptions—especially regarding what a child is and how human beings learn—that we have outgrown. What's needed, not only in kindergarten but also in postgraduate education, is to have schools become what other organizations are learning to be: learning organizations, adapting to changes in the world around them and equipping those they serve for the world that's just around the corner.

Change Comes Hard

Colleges are difficult organizations to change. And we know that colleges have gotten a lot larger and more unwieldy in the last century. In 1920 the average four-year institution had 457 enrolled students and the average two-year college had 154. In 1980 these numbers had swelled from 457 to 4,070 and from 154 to 3,604. Even this doesn't tell the whole story because over the past 20 years more than half of all college and university students, and nearly half of all professors, were in the 10% of institutions that enroll more than 10,000 students. Institutions of such magnitude carry with them a critical mass that resists change in uncountable ways.

Even within small institutions, however, the weight of tradition is leveraged against every appeal for change. Colleges and universities are exemplars of what Mary Douglas saw in all sorts of institutions: " . . . there are four decisive arguments in organizational change: there is no time; it is unnatural; God prohibits it; and there is no money" (qtd. in Keller, 1983, p. 57). We have, most of us, experienced a thousand variations on those themes. And we shall hear them again each time we propose to revamp collegiate models and programs to match the realities of a learning age.

The organizational orthodoxy of our colleges and universities is stifling creative responses to a changing environment. There's a rising tide of new knowledge about the way people learn. This knowledge has not yet permeated the American educational process. And we are developing technological capacity that boggles the mind. Yet we lag in using it to support learning. Simultaneously, we face a flood of new students who, because they are Americans, expect the right to earn a degree, to come to the table of opportunity. Until we come to grips with how people learn and adapt our practices to meet their needs, we will be unable as a nation to reinvigorate the promise of opportunity that has been ours for more than two centuries.

We need Margery Moore's practical vision and call to authenticity. We need to offer the whole loaf, to finish the job of making real educational opportunity available to all. In Jefferson's terms, we are at a point in our growth where we need a new wardrobe—not just a bigger set of the old clothes, but a whole new fashion line. Unlike the challenge that Margery threw down, today's struggle is not simply to achieve credits for learning but to reshape the learning itself. Higher education in America has not responded to the knowledge or technologies or cultures or futures that have already remolded the lives of millions of Americans as well as most American business. There's a reason Peter Senge is better known at Motorola than in our schools of education.

Changing Institutions of Learning

Tension is increasing between the traditional structures of universities on the one hand and the American expectation that higher education is the right of all qualified citizens on the other. Some of this tension emanates from a deepening challenge to our traditional structures and policies. Universities see themselves as keepers of tradition. But some of what's described as tradition is not worthy of being kept. It is, in fact, bad habit and accumulated ignorance. Our colleges and universities have frequently proven Peter Drucker's (1999) claim that institutions are designed for continuity, and, therefore, resistant to change. Drucker stated that changing the traditional institution is a contradiction in terms, and no institution is more traditional than the ivy-clad university.

So what are we to do? Within our universities, we should pay attention to establishing cultures of evidence that give us authentic information on how successful we are at the things we say are important. We ask students to be accountable for their work. We need to be accountable for ours.

Every institution has a mission statement and a strategic plan. And every institution has a research office that develops institutional data for reports. That function, largely ignored in the daily life of most colleges and universities, needs to be exhumed and placed at the center of a quality assurance effort that connects the objectives of the strategic plan to the actual performance of the institution. We need to find out how well we do at the things that we say are important, that matter to us. And if the answer is "not that well" then we need to look for better ways.

In *Good to Great*, James Collins (2001) reveals that one of the core characteristics of high-performing institutions is a willingness to ask the most difficult questions and to successfully address the problems they raise. In other words, high performance organizations are willing to bring the drunken uncle out of the closet. Although the questions might vary from institution to institution, here are a few to get you started (Flint & Associates, 1999).

- Are the administrative and academic practices of the college learner-focused?
- Do you treat each person like an individual and a valued customer?
- Why do students leave?
- What do they say about the climate for teaching and learning? The quality of teaching? The academic support?
- What actual data, not stories and anecdotes, do you have on the effectiveness of your teaching, climate, practices, and support?
- Does every student have a learning profile that includes his or her prior educational history, learning style, and multiple intelligence profile? Do you use it in a diagnostic process to align educational resources with needs?
- What is the relationship of tenure to quality teaching and learning? Of departmental structures to cross-curricular preparation?
- How well does the university incorporate the resources of the community as learning resources for students?

- Is academic performance built on well-prepared
  and aggressive students or a curricular structure and
  approaches to teaching and learning that bring out the
  strengths in every person?
- Do first-generation students persist and graduate at the
  same rates of others?

At the societal level, we must ask the same questions of the
interface between the higher education system and the society. What
are our goals? What does the evidence tell us about our success? What
can we do differently and better to improve our impact?

In the lobby of the Woodrow Wilson School of Public and
International Affairs at Princeton University stands a sculpture. At first
glance it looks like a metallic sea urchin covered with spines ready to
fend off any enemy's threat. But if you look closer you discover that the
spines are not weapons of defense. On the contrary, they are reeds that
when any one of them quivers, all will vibrate. The sculpture is a model
of interdependence and connectedness. The artist's point: In the affairs
of countries and diplomacy, as in life, we are all interconnected. What
happens to one of us affects all of us. We cannot operate in isolation
and be effective.

Unless we are successfully serving those who truly represent the
communities we serve—no matter what their grouping by age or race
or ethnicity or economics—we are disconnected from our own life
sources. Unless our pedagogy is aligned with the intellectual profile
of our learners as well as the actual needs of employers, unless our
perspectives are at least as global and fluid as the world economy, and
unless our accountability is high and public, we will not be able to
survive, let alone succeed. Education is a servant to opportunity. And
when the consequence of our work is not more opportunity but less,
we will no longer have a role to play in the life of our community.

A vast amount of learning happens today within business.
Corporations fund their own learning in large part because they have
no choice. Those they've hired do not have the skills, knowledge, or
perspective needed for the business to compete effectively in a global
market. And business and labor, working together through groups like

the Council for Adult and Experiential Learning (CAEL), are building workplace-based programs that meet the needs of the workers (as learners) as well as the employers. For those of us in education—whether our involvement is as a parent or student, a member of a local school board, or a professor in a famed university—a powerful lesson is here for the taking. Learning will not disappear. But we may. And already we have proven largely irrelevant to many we claim to be serving.

If a society or an organization must change but cannot—because its culture, organizational structure, and tradition hold it too tightly in place—then that culture or organization is doomed. Thomas Kuhn (1962) discussed such doomed institutions in *The Structure of Scientific Revolutions*. The first instinct of tradition, he noted, is to repel new thoughts that rest on different assumptions. So, for example, the challenge of Aristotle's teaching, Newton's physics, or Luther's reformation were all violently resisted, rejected because they violated the known order of the world. Over time the newly observed phenomenon gathers more evidence and eventually takes its place within a renewed tradition. It may take a decade, or it may take a century, but finally new knowledge takes hold and the keepers of tradition change. So change happens. But it takes almost forever. And forever is not an option available to America or American higher education today.

Barriers to Change
Whether we're citing Kuhn or quoting Drucker or recalling Senge, schools and colleges must become learning organizations capable of balancing tradition and change. Although their destinies are an integral part of the society around them, mutually reinforced, in many cases we have built institutions of higher learning in isolation from the rest of the world. The traditional university draws great strength from the protections it gives scholarship, the security it gives students and alumni, and the research relationships it forms with business and government. But the institutions themselves seem largely incapable of adopting the knowledge they have created about learning. Nations have risen and fallen more quickly than our institutions of learning have changed.

Government is another part of the problem. Federal and state legislation often promotes lofty goals while providing no means of paying for them. Politicians attempt to balance competing interests—between universities, for example, that want more funding of tomorrow's research and businesses that want capable employees today. But this balanced approach ignores the dysfunctional structure of schools, perpetuating the status quo and treating universities more like the constituent bodies they are than the societal servants they should be. A growing chorus of voices is demanding a role in policies governing higher education: our mission, our delivery system, and our destiny. They don't trust us to deliver anymore, believing that we are either ignoring their urgent demands or denying the truth of what we hear.

We've risen to this kind of educational challenge before. Amid the Cold War, Sputnik, and the Great Society, our nation witnessed a dramatic increase in government's commitment to education at all levels. We focused on access and equity, and we made great progress.

And in the 1980s Secretary of Education Terrell Bell became increasingly concerned about the declining performance of America's students, so he created a departmental commission to study the problem. His blockbuster report, "A Nation at Risk," sent shock waves through the country and became the foundation for two decades of commitment to education reform in America. Yet the same 20 years have also been marked by the paralysis of partisanship in Washington. With divided government, and even greater ideological divides over the role of the federal government in education, little progress was made.

Many believe a similar focus on access and accountability will become the basis for review of our higher education partnership with government in the future. Neither our nation nor our higher education community can afford a similar stalemate in the effort to reform postsecondary education.

The test of all education, and especially higher education, is our ability to successfully generate high-quality learning not for the few but for the many. If you look behind the numbers, we haven't been that successful even with relatively small traditional populations of students over the last 40 years.

We've provided ever-increasing access to a college education, but we have been much less successful at finishing the job, graduating students prepared for life. We're doing better at giving people chairs at the table of opportunity, but we're not doing better at providing any real nutrition once they've taken their seats.

Our educational systems have been impressively slow in recognizing the relationship between learning and culture. Learning, like talking, is culturally conditioned. Some cultures encourage conversations that are soft and indirect; others promote talk that's loud, inches from your nose. To move from one culture to the other can be hugely painful. And learning is as culturally conditioned as talking. Still, our institutions of learning persist in thinking that education is a garment cut one size to fit all.

The Challenge for Higher Education in the 21st Century

Here's where we find ourselves as we enter the great debates about higher education in the opening hours of the 21st century:

- We know that today's world has very different standards for success.
- We know that today's students are different people representing different demographics and cultures.
- We know that today's students learn in many different ways.
- We know that technology now allows us to both better understand how people learn and to design learning systems that fit the uniqueness of each student.

We know a great deal about learners and learning. Yet, all too often, our colleges and universities—and the public policy guiding them—block the very changes in learning they should be leading. If America is going to get on its learning curve, professional educators, critical policymakers, parents, and business leaders must help us reinvent our colleges and universities so they are based on how people learn, not how we wish we could teach them.

Colleges and universities can help lead this effort by embracing commitments to excellence such as the Malcolm Baldridge Award for education, a rigorous continuous renewal program that is employed in both the public and private sectors. Some colleges, like University of Wisconsin–Stout, have taken on this challenge successfully. In 2002, UW-Stout, a relatively small campus (8,000 students) in western Wisconsin, became the first college or university in America to win the Baldridge Award for Excellence. As part of its application for this award, the University of Wisconsin–Stout conducted a visioning session for its future. Its chancellor, Charles Sorensen, assembled a large group of leaders from education, business, industry, and government to identify the long-term strategic direction for the university in service to its students and faculty, its alumni, business and industry, and the citizens and communities of the region. In many ways, this initiative put a modern face on the historic concept of "The Wisconsin Idea," where its public university system serves the greater good of the state through its programs in education. Among its recommendations, this visioning session identified 10 possible directions for consideration in the decade ahead, half of which might apply broadly in other settings (The Greystone Group, 2001):

- Establishing itself as a premier institution in workforce preparation
- Becoming a national clearinghouse for workforce preparation
- Creating a "Center for Workplace Learning"
- Creating a "Convenience University"
- Creating an "Alumni Skills Guarantee," and others

This type of vision, combined with a vigorous commitment to serving the community and supported by a culture of evidence and a commitment to continuous improvement, must become the trademark for higher education. While I suspect UW-Stout will seek both public and private resources to support its initiatives in reaching out to the greater community, I am struck by how the vision was conceived by the university to enhance its service to the community—not to secure government approval as the condition for additional funding.

I once heard a speaker entreat an audience of skeptical businessmen, "If I can't appeal to your hearts, let me appeal to your wallets." He was talking about the need for an educated citizenry and workforce as essential elements in America's survival as a representative democracy. And he was right. We must find ways to educate people throughout life who can think, who can learn, and who can work. And the academic tradition, like the initial model proposed for the Community College of Vermont, is only half of the loaf for millions of learners.

The world is changing around us. As it changes, so do the rules. We have grown up with the belief that tradition—stability and the repetition of known and unchanging things—is the key to success. This is a belief grounded on the assumption of minimal or incremental change. One step at a time. Considered. Certain. Understood. It worked because the tradition reflected the pace of movement and change in the country at large. But the pace of change has accelerated dramatically.

Roberts Jones of the National Alliance of Business once quoted a business colleague who had suggested that if the rate of change outside your organization exceeded the rate of change inside your organization, the end might be in sight (Jones, 2002). Jones articulated the business view of changes facing higher education, suggesting that

> . . . higher education has an obligation to become more responsive to rising demands for certain types of degrees; more inclusive at a time when all students must attain higher levels of academic proficiency; more user-friendly to accommodate the rising importance of lifelong learning; and more capable of communicating student competencies at a time when shifting skill demands have diminished the reliability of institutional prestige. In addition, the time has come to fashion a funding mechanism adequate to an age when all people will have to return to the postsecondary system repeatedly throughout their lives. (Jones, 2002, p. 10)

If Jones is right, America's current systems of education cannot succeed at the job that faces them.

Conclusion: Leading a Reform

Senator Justin Morrill brought America through a fork in the road 140 years ago when he successfully proposed establishing land-grant universities to reach out to the common man and the businesses of the communities, including agriculture. He knew that America could not prosper without a broader role for American colleges and universities.

One hundred and fifty years after Justin Morrill, America has come to another fork in the road in its understanding of education's importance and educational opportunity. In one direction lies the path of most educational reform proposed since 1980. We have witnessed two decades of strident rhetoric by those advocating reform, and defensive responses by those protecting our traditional education delivery systems. All may have meant well. None were very constructive.

In the other direction lies a learning society, with millions of Americans new to education and opportunity, bringing their traditions and cultures as well as their hopes and aspirations to the table of opportunity. It could be America's finest and most exciting hour in defining the role, relevance, and relationship of education to society. It simply depends upon which path we choose.

Our choice will ultimately depend in large measure on our leaders. Leadership is not easy. The price can be, and sometimes is, very high. School board members asked to vote on issues that will raise the cost of education or change its form may do so at risk of their seat at the board table. Members of Congress must balance loyalty to party leaders with commitment to their constituents. And within the systems of education, among the so-called professional educators, leadership is muted by a thousand calls to caution.

I know the temptations to dream large and act small. They are my own. I've heard the quote often attributed to Napoleon, "I should rather have an army of rabbits led by a lion than an army of lions led by a rabbit." We don't need rabbits for this struggle. We need an army of lions, and for our leaders—at the community, institutional, state, and federal levels—to show the heart of lions as well.

When I ask myself "Where will we get these leaders?" I am

reminded of the old story told in Maine about two men who went up to Blue Hill for a visit. While they were there, they went to the Blue Hill Fair. A man was selling hot-air balloon rides, so they bought one and were soon drifting over the countryside of Maine. After a long time, longer than they had planned on, they landed in a farmer's pasture. The old fellow leaned on his hoe. "Howdy," he said. One of the strangers leaned over the edge of the balloon basket and said, "Excuse me, sir, but do you know where we are?" And the farmer replied, "You're in a balloon, you damn fool."

To find our leaders we need to look in the mirror: graduate students who train to become tomorrow's professors and administrators; policymakers and politicians who aspire to lead, not simply serve; parents and students who need to look beyond the special interest of their own educational experience to the larger need, understanding how it affects them; and educational entrepreneurs who want to test new models. There is a choice to be made as each of these people approaches the fork in the road. Each needs to ask, "Will I work toward, or support, institutions that serve the historic perspective of higher education? Or will I prepare to serve in and support organizations that bridge to the future, harnessing the new forces and knowledge, serving the new learners, and learning continuously how to adapt to achieve future excellence?"

If we are to keep the American promise to the real America, the one whose population is increasingly diverse and whose economy is increasingly global, we will need leaders with courage as well as vision, knowledge as well as passion, and grace under the fire which is likely to come from many of the very institutions that are most in need of change.

3

▼

BREAKING THE MODEL: FROM STORIED TRADITION TO VALUED POSITION

Twenty-five years ago, on a cold February night, I sat at a kitchen table in an old Vermont farmhouse enjoying the warmth of the nearby wood stove. Our neighbors had asked me to come over. They wanted to talk about their daughter going to college. They needed help with the forms. Armand cut stone at the local quarry. He was a good man who worked hard and earned enough for his family to get by. Barbara, his wife, had health problems but she was able to raise their three girls on a combination of affection, ingenuity, and New England thrift. They lived on the family farm, 30-some acres of dry rocks and marshy lowland. It was an old hill farm. It had never been very productive and it had been lying fallow for some time. But it was theirs. And the land, the house, and the family shared an identity of hard work, neighborly compassion, and unassuming decency. When the fields gave out, Armand never complained; he went to work in the quarry, grateful for the opportunity.

Armand and Barbara had decided that one of their daughters, Nicole, should go to college. No one in his or her family had done this before. It was an historic first. And though they never said so, it was their way of saying, "We want a better future for her." It was a painful decision, breaking the tradition; it felt to them as if they were losing her. What would she become when she knew what they did not know, when she was educated. Would she be ashamed of this place, these people? Would she put on airs? In the end, they decided, it didn't matter. They wanted her to have an opportunity no one else in the family had had, the opportunity to do better.

I had warmed myself on their wood stove many times before. When I had chaired the local school board, I'd pulled up a kitchen chair to make the case for higher taxes to support better schools. Armand and Barbara were my community barometers: If they could agree to pay more, others would too. I remembered saying to them that good schools were worth "the price of a six pack of beer a week" to each family in the town. They'd agreed. They'd also believed me when I said, "If you ever want Nicole to consider college, let me know. I'll help."

Armand and Barbara were, with other poor and working couples in that New England community, the reason our schools went from last in the district to first. They embraced the vision of better schools, they believed in it, and they were willing to pay for it. Now, it was time to settle accounts. They wanted Nicole to go to college. It was time for me to support their vision.

Nicole was bright. My wife, Sally, had been her first-grade teacher. Nicole had excelled at every level; she'd been a Candy Stripe volunteer in the local hospital; she'd led church and 4-H groups. She was what colleges were looking for. Besides, by the time we'd worked through the forms together, we knew that Armand and Barbara qualified for full financial aid. The next fall Nicole enrolled as a nursing student in the college of her dreams. When she left, she shook her father's hand and gave her mother a hug. There were no tears. Not in this home. Not on this farm. Not until they were, each of them, alone.

Nicole, alone and away, easily mastered college classes. But she had more trouble with college life. She longed for the smell of that kitchen, the dry warmth of the wood stove, the sound of her mother's voice. That distant farm seemed rich and fragrant; the college campus was gray, barren. She wrote letters that hinted at her unhappiness; Barbara responded, urging her to "hang on a bit," "stick it out a little," "it's only a few months before summer . . . " Nicole did not want to disappoint her parents. They had given her this gift. But she could not endure it. The sparkle dried in her eyes. Her stomach hurt. She walked the campus looking down, speaking to no one, noticed by few.

And then, one day, she wasn't there anymore. She left. Eventually she recovered some hope, she married, got a job, had a baby, and moved onto a farm. She believed, however, that she had failed the family. Armand and Barbara, meanwhile, believed that they had failed their daughter. They just weren't quite sure what they had done wrong.

I have known for two and a half decades that any failure here was not Nicole's or Armand's or Barbara's. It was the college's failure. The family did not fail the student, and the student did not fail the college; the college failed them all.

And I have also known for two and a half decades that, in a real sense, I failed them all. I could, and should, have done more than fill out forms at that worn kitchen table. I knew what that college campus was like, and what these good people were like. What was I thinking? Why didn't I speak up? How could I have been a party to this tragedy?

Although every family's and student's college experience is unique, failure to thrive is as much a condition on college campuses today as ever. Roughly half of those who enroll in college graduate within five years. About 60% will eventually get a degree. This means that 40% who enroll in college never reach graduation. In the 21st century, this will matter, a lot.

I work in California's Monterey County, balanced between Monterey, Pebble Beach, and Carmel on the one hand and the Salinas Valley on the other. Colleagues of mine at California State University–Monterey Bay go into the region's elementary and middle schools to assure the children of agricultural workers that our university is their university, that we'll be here when they are ready and eligible. We bring this message because we believe that educating all of our children and workers to high standards is rooted in the promise of opportunity planted by our nation's founders.

Access to College Is More Than Admission

As anyone who does it knows, however, creating access to college is a "one student at a time" effort that can extend for 10 or more years. It begins with building the expectation and confidence, as early as the sixth grade, that college is there for them—psychologically, socially, and financially. It extends through the high school years, with support, mentoring, and exposure to college programs and campuses. And, after admission, it includes helping parents to say goodbye to children leaving for a new life, creating intellectual and psychological support, as well as academic encouragement, for pioneer learners who are the first in their families to push out into the educational wilderness. And, as professionals, we know that every student is unique, coming with their own strengths and weaknesses as they enter our institution.

Too often, however, we confuse newness to higher education, being the first in your family or coming from a low-income background, with weakness in the individual. So our approach is remedial, to fix the new learners, trimming their edges to fit them into our institution and tradition, instead of building our learning programs around their strengths. And so, unwittingly, as we try to do the right thing, setting high standards and asking for good work, we emphasize the wrong thing, alienating students from their cultures, their backgrounds, their histories, and their strengths. Higher education administrators and faculty, other leaders, and citizens alike must focus less on the risks and more on the assets that diversity represents; we must learn from the rich hues of culture, experience, and perspective. We must acknowledge that different people learn in different ways. And when we imagine the American table of opportunity, we should think of a gigantic Thanksgiving feast celebrated by Hispanic field workers as well as Calvinist pilgrims, Vietnamese refugees, and descendants of slaves. Our colleges and universities need to successfully educate and graduate that same diversity.

As a college president, I am accountable for a place where parents send their Nicoles and Bobs. I can look out my window and see students of every economic and ethnic and religious group; if I open the window, I will hear English and Spanish and Chinese and probably Hmong. When I drive by our local hospital, whose CEO is a friend, I sometimes wonder what our community would say if four out of ten people admitted to this hospital were not successfully treated? Would we blame the patients for failing to be healthy? Would I ever suggest that Sally or the children seek treatment there? And what if my community held me accountable for learning the way I hold my CEO friend accountable for healing?

This is where the myth of college opportunity collides head-on with the brutal reality our children have faced for years. Colleges are bridges to opportunity, but they are also social filters removing nearly half of all who attend. We offer opportunity, but on our own terms— and our terms are sink or swim. About half tread water and many of them sink. Along with the success stories, many of those who manage to swim all the way to graduation are survivors. They have escaped with a degree.

Too often, however, the missing footnote in college recruitment materials is that learning will be the responsibility of the student. If truth in advertising were applied to recruitment mailings, they would be headlined, "Success here is your business, not ours." "We'll take care of the teaching; you will be held accountable for the learning." "We'll set costs and standards; you'll pay for both."

I have enjoyed and profited from extraordinary teachers during my lifetime: my parents; three or four elementary and high school teachers; a professor and a graduate school professor, still a friend. But the lesson that changed my career was taught by three good people in Vermont: parents who wanted something better for their daughter and their daughter who wanted not to disappoint her family. Together, they changed my expectations for higher education. They changed my goals.

The Leaky Campus

The classic model of higher education in America has come into the 21st century largely unchanged. We remember musty classrooms with tenured, wise men and women standing before classes of students paying thousands of dollars per year to drink in knowledge. Outside the class, on an autumn afternoon, the marching band rehearses for Saturday's football game. Older buildings across campus are dressed in ivy and history; new buildings wear bold letters spelling out the names of major donors. Give or take a detail, this is the common vision of American higher education.

But the problem with this vision isn't how it looks. It's how it works. And it doesn't work well. It doesn't serve the needs of many of our students, their families, the surrounding communities, or employers. American higher education weeds out those it should nurture. It resists the technology that can broaden its reach, speed its service, enhance its learning, and decrease its costs. It protects a teaching method that ignores what we know about how students learn best.

If the goal of a college is to be well thought of by other colleges; if the president of a college wants to move up to even more prestigious, high-paying jobs; if the aim is to enroll only the wealthiest, smartest, and most promising students who have already demonstrated their capacity for academic work; this model serves pretty well. It will weed out those not ready, but it won't identify their intelligence and interests and support their learning. It will teach cutthroat competition to faculty and students. But it won't teach teamwork. It will produce a few extraordinary alumni whose faces will decorate future college catalogs and whose names will eventually be mounted on new campus buildings. But their success will be standing on the shoulders of many who failed. If the goal of a college, however, is to serve its community and nation by equipping students and graduates to be socially, economically, and civilly competitive in a global society, this model must be revamped.

In this sense, American higher education is like the *Titanic*. It is the best ever. Constructed to create and perpetuate knowledge and open to millions of new learners who didn't have access before, our colleges and universities are the envy of the world. They are growing, robust, and deeply respected.

And people like me, who are privileged to lead a college, are like the captain of the *Titanic*. We're professionals, presumably good at what we're trained and hired to do. We believe that we have earned the right, through scholarship and research and sweat, to help lead the best system known to the world. We are alert and concerned for the welfare of all who come on board, faculty, staff, and students alike. We are proud of our role in society and sure of our vision.

The *Titanic* had various classes of service, comfort, and cost. All passengers would arrive at the same destination but some would travel in upper-deck splendor while others would not. Some paid more, ate better, took brandy with cigars in the salon. Others endured more cramped quarters and suffered seasickness. But all were on the boat, going to the same place.

Colleges have a parallel caste system. For example, today nearly every state offers automatic entry into its public universities for students who were valedictorians of their high school graduating class. This is a perfectly good idea. It typically originates in the state legislature or governor's mansion as a way of keeping the state's smartest, or at least most academically successful, kids at home. But it has little to do with preparing the citizenry to meet the needs of today or tomorrow. Those who have been successful will succeed again living, one might say, on the upper decks of higher education. Meanwhile, late Friday night we will find the daughter of immigrants and the son of an impoverished single parent mopping floors in the cafeteria kitchen. They travel in the engine room where it is hot and grimy.

I realize the danger in such analogies. But I will risk this one, because our future depends on being successful with the people who are below deck: the unknowns, those who never get to campus, those who walk across campus yet-to-be-discovered without scholarships, and those who never win the beauty contests and athletic awards. Those least likely to appeal to fraternities and sororities, least likely to be popular on campus, are those with whom we must do our best. To have a society that is socially, civically, and economically vital, we need more than a head table at the banquet. We need everyone at a table, valued enough to be hopeful, comfortable enough to endure, learning enough to succeed.

The United States entered this century trailing Norway, Great Britain, and the Netherlands in the proportion of population graduating from college; other nations are poised to surpass us on this list (and likely have by the time you read this). How is this possible?

> While American postsecondary enrollments grew at an average annual rate of 1.1 percent between 1980 and 1997, for example, Chinese and Indonesian annual en-rollment growth reached 15.6 percent and 19.1 per-

cent, respectively. At these rates, enrollment levels in
such countries may well exceed American levels within
decades. (Jones, 2002, p. 10)

Even before Hollywood had its way with the *Titanic*, its voyage
was a story full of crisis and drama. No such drama has attached to
American higher education as it has slowly, inexorably failed to achieve
the level of excellence and learning that must be the watermark for our
performance. No iceberg fields lurk before colleges on a dark night in
the North Atlantic. Do not look for the story of Armand, Barbara, and
Nicole on HBO next week. Our failing students don't die dramatic
deaths; they merely slip away, uncounted until we add up their numbers
and see that roughly 40% of those who got on board did not make it
to graduation. And that's on top of those who failed to graduate from
high school! And—here's a difference from the *Titanic* example—in
colleges and universities, the institution is not at fault; I, as president,
am blameless. The traditional model of college tells us all that it is the
students who have failed, not the college. They bear the shame.

If we continue to advertise that higher education promises
opportunity for all who will commit to it, our problem is not the
iceberg. We are sailing a sea of failure and hypocrisy. Dr. Clifford
Adelman (1999) recently completed a study of the factors that most
highly determined a student's success in college. His findings are
ominous because the two most determinative factors are academic
performance and preparation, meaning what students bring with them
to college from high school, and continuous enrollment, meaning
once they begin higher education they do not take a break. But most
students take more than four years and many of them do take a break.
Considered another way, Adelman's findings say that we don't control
the first factor of success, high school preparation, and we have failed
to adjust for success with a more mobile student body. Finally, what
he doesn't say, and what hurts the most, is that the quality of what we
do with our teaching and learning in universities is not a top factor in
student success.

Such research doesn't grab us by the throat like the sound of wailing drowning victims. I admit it. Maybe American higher education isn't like the *Titanic* so much as it's like the boiling frog. The tradition has been comfortable, so there's been no reason for us to jump out of the pot. As the temperature around us has risen, we've yawned and stretched and grown sluggish and sleepy. We're willing to lean back and be boiled. Why? "Because the frog's internal apparatus for sensing threats to survival is geared to sudden changes in his environment, not to slow, gradual changes" (Senge, 1990, p. 22).

Inclusive Learning Versus Exclusive Teaching

Senge's favorite application of the boiled frog parable is the U.S. auto industry. In 1962, Japanese car builders had less than a 4% share of the U.S. market. By 1967, it was approaching 10%, by 1974, 15%. By the early 1980s Japan owned more than 20% of the U.S. market (Handy, 1989).

How did this happen? For decades American car manufacturers liked to answer the question, "What shall we give our customers?" While Detroit decided what it wanted to produce, auto executives from Tokyo asked a different question: "What do American customers want?" The question from Tokyo was smarter.

For decades—well, actually, for centuries—schools have been deciding what they would teach and how students would learn. On the learning curve, higher education needs to answer a new question: How do we put learning at the center? This one insight is the platform to revolutionize colleges and universities from the Atlantic to the Pacific. It changes the star of the show from the person being paid to the person paying, from the professor to the student, from what was taught to how well it was learned. It revamps the criteria by which a board of trustees or system chancellor evaluates presidents, provosts, and deans. It will, rapidly and dramatically, throw us into the arms of technology where we will find power, speed, and cost savings. It might even—though I admit that this is improbable—make learning as important as basketball.

If we are going to make the transition from a storied tradition to a valued position, those who shape and lead higher education will need to focus on learning beyond what our campuses provide. We need to ask the learning questions in concert with our communities and in partnership with all the institutions that are, today, purveyors of higher education in America: corporations, churches, professional associations, research and consulting firms, and community groups, to name a few. We should make an honest assessment of how much innovation in learning is being done by others simply because we have failed to do it ourselves. And we should note with concern the lack of alignment between the structure and traditions of colleges and the needs of the society that supports us.

Donna Queeney's thoughtful 1996 paper on this very subject challenged higher education to take the lead in creating a learning society that encourages, values, and rewards consistent lifelong learning. And she suggests no fewer than 16 strategies for higher education, including listening to society's interests and demands for such education and making a compact with the university's students to serve their lifelong learning needs (Queeney, 1996).

Conclusion: Devotion to Learning

For years, colleges have been both gateways to opportunity and filters removing less successful learners from the stream of graduates. Very few other social institutions define success as much by how many fail as by who succeeds. This is where the promise of opportunity has broken down, because colleges have not taken institutional responsibility for successful learning. If learners leave, it's their choice. If they fail, it's their fault.

We cannot continue with this set of assumptions. There is too much need and too much capacity for learning. If, instead, American higher education actually devoted itself to learning—to equipping people of all races and ages and interests to becoming social, economic, and civil contributors in our society—then we would harness the synergy offered by demography, technology, and new knowledge and develop a new ethos of education for the 21st century.

PART TWO
THE EMERGENCE OF A NEW LEARNING ETHOS

4

▼

LIVED EXPERIENCE:
THE ROOT OF LEARNING

I was raised in the American era of the 1950s where the structure and purposes of education were almost universally admired and accepted. In any dispute between teacher and student, the teacher was always on the side of the angels. And the rules in college were simple: They teach, you learn. Your formal education was the pathway to success. College was the platform from which one could dive into a successful life of work, service, and contribution. "Get your education" and everything else will follow. But we are outgrowing the assumptions inherent in the old model, that knowledge is something fixed and static, that it can be accumulated and held by those who choose to pursue formal education.

Over the last half of the 20th century, America began to generate a new learning ethos. Since the end of World War II, we have witnessed staggering expansion in the number of colleges and in our knowledge about learning. Here are just a few examples of new knowledge about learning that have been useful for me as I have grappled with the problems associated with reorganizing universities for learning.

- Dr. Allen Tough began to define and describe informal learning with his book, *The Adult's Learning Projects: A*

Fresh Approach to Theory and Practice in Adult Learning (1971).

- A bit more than a decade later, in 1983, Howard Gardner authored *Frames of Mind* in which he began to develop his theory of multiple intelligences that bridge cultural perspectives on human learning.
- Similarly, Barry Sheckley and Morris Keeton (2001) have advanced the concept of learning retention, the relationship between how something is learned, and how long the learner can remember and apply it.
- Carol Gilligan (1982) and Mary Belenky (1997) provided valuable insights into emerging differences between the genders in moral and psychological development and the interpretation of experience.
- Mary Meeker (1969) developed the Structure of Intellect (SOI) paradigm, working with multiple intelligences.

As these examples suggest, we have learned more about learning since 1950 than we did in all the preceding years.

Most of the evidence that we've accumulated about the way people learn contradicts traditional common practice about teaching and learning. It does not support the traditional academic model of colleges and universities. We know that although each person might approach learning differently, all people learn from their lived experience, including the experience of school. And we know that formal education that engages that experience and the learner will be more effective.

Yet sadly, precisely because much of this emerging knowledge challenges the historic structure of universities, we ignore it. Higher education has treated new and valued knowledge about why people learn and how they learn best like the modern doctor who, seeing a badly infected toe, calls for a bullet and a saw. Most colleges and universities operate like an emergency room where the first thing they do is put a splint on your arm, regardless of your complaint. Imagine the conversation:

"What happened to you?"

"My head and neck are killing me. I was whiplashed when my car was rear-ended."

"OK, let's just get this splint on your arm, and then we'll talk."

Absurd? Absolutely. Despite our best intentions, however, this approximates the standard MO in most of our colleges and universities. We have organized American higher education—from classroom architecture to graduation standards—around the interests of the university, not the needs and the learning profile of the student. We've built our systems and our structures largely on a traditional, academic, one-size-fits-all model instead of being responsive to the learning, experiences, and characteristics of students. We teach the curriculum, thus meeting the needs of the college because teaching the student would be terribly inconvenient and disorienting. In American higher education, too often, we apply the splint first and ask questions later.

When I was eight or nine my grandfather would read to me on Sunday afternoons in the winter. I can remember sitting in his living room, listening and talking in front of a comforting fire. One afternoon, he looked down over his reading glasses and assured me that "life is the school of hard knocks," that "you live and you learn." I believed him in these matters, as I believed him in all others.

But what my grandfather didn't know was that there was more than mythology and his personal experience backing up his belief that you would become "older, but wiser." In 1955, he couldn't have known because the research hadn't been done then. Ten years after our Sabbath conversation, Dr. Allen Tough's research on learning projects enabled him first to identify and then to describe how and why individuals actually go about learning through the experience of living.

Individual Learning
Tough (1971) defined a learning project as a concerted effort to learn a new behavior, skill, or knowledge that lasted at least 12 to 15 hours. As he

studied the phenomenon of learning projects, he discovered that people everywhere, across continents, cultures, and lifestyles, regardless of income and education level, are involved continuously in these learning projects. The average person conducted eight to ten such projects running from a low of one to a high of over thirty each year of their adulthood.

Over time, Tough was able to fill out the picture of this natural but purposeful and focused learning that people do all the time. What he learned and then proved is that without assistance the learner sets a goal and then decides what she or he needs to learn, how best to achieve that learning, and when enough learning has occurred. Sometimes with the aid of a mentor, often proceeding alone, learners then would go to the library, seek out an expert, or ask help from peers. Today, a learner would be equally likely to search the web as the most common portal of information and knowledge. What Tough demonstrated is that we all begin, pursue, and conclude these projects without prompting from formal educational systems.

Learning is an individual affair. We may learn in groups, with groups, about groups, and even for groups. But we learn as individuals. It happens inside the skin of people, one at a time. This may be obvious when stated but it is often obscured by our tendency to organize learning around and through groups.

The learning society cannot be built around technology or colleges. They are tools, mechanisms. It is built on individual people who are learners. Tip O'Neill, the legendary speaker of the U.S. House of Representatives, wrote in his 1994 memoirs, "All politics is local." So it is. Equally true is that all learning is individual. Each individual's learning becomes, when introduced to our shared communities, one element of the formal and informal learning society.

Individual learning has three important characteristics (Smith, 1986):

- **It is always personal.** Learning is shaped to and by our uniqueness. One person is moved to tears upon learning the story of Abraham Lincoln's childhood; another yawns. A young woman, recently orphaned, reads a psychology text in ways a retired autoworker,

returned to college for a few classes, cannot imagine—
and the inverse is equally true. One person's revelation
about culture and diversity is another's confirmation.
We learn as we are, influenced by our fears and our
faith and our singular experiences.

- **It is always purposeful**. Learning happens because
  we want it to. We read and remember the essence of a
  passage because it explains our life a little bit, we think
  it's perceptive, and we want to quote it to someone else.
  We admire a skill or resource someone else has, and
  want to learn it ourselves. We may forget why we first
  started; we may shift what we value most; but if we are
  in fact learning, it is because we, as individuals, want
  and need to learn.

- **It is always powerful**. Learning, unlike nearly anything
  else, bears down on us in ways that change us: it revises
  how we think, how we feel, how we behave. It yields
  new skills with which we can surprise or delight others
  and ourselves. It enables us to rise above our place
  in society by showing others our unique, hidden
  credentials. Even if we are not thinking about what we
  are doing as learning—checking an old recipe in a worn
  cookbook, reading a journal, seeing a counselor—it is,
  in fact, what we are doing.

We may quibble over terminology, but we need a word that
represents the basic building block for our personal learning. It could
be a lesson or a unit, but those words connote classrooms and formal
structures that do not fit most settings at home or at work. Allen Tough
suggested a better term: projects. As described earlier, learning projects
are intentional efforts in which we set out to learn. Think, for example,
of learning how to canoe for the first time, reading up on attention
deficit disorder or alcoholism to better understand your own frustrations
or someone else's, or undertaking to master the piano well enough to

surprise your wife with her favorite song on your anniversary. Tough (1971) describes these fundamental units in his landmark *The Adult's Learning Projects.*

> Almost everyone undertakes at least one or two major learning projects a year. Some people undertake as many as fifteen or twenty. The median is eight projects a year lasting a total of eight hundred hours (15 hours a week) . . . Highly deliberate learning efforts take place all around you. The members of your family, your neighbors, colleagues, and acquaintances probably initiate and complete several learning projects each year . . . When asked about their learning efforts, many of our interviewees recalled none at first, but as the interview proceeded, they recalled several recent efforts to learn. (pp. 13–14)

American folklore is filled with phrases and anecdotes like "live and learn," "trial and error," and "the school of hard knocks." Each phrase suggests that what we know is a product of what we've experienced. In a sense, that's what Tough is confirming. Without truly experiencing something and reflecting on it, we cannot learn. When we do learn, we will change.

The pedagogical insights to be drawn from pioneering research such as Tough's reconfigure the landscape of the traditional teaching-learning model. His research suggests that learning happens naturally and continuously, occurring when there is a strong connection between "it" (whatever is to be learned) and "me" (the lived experience of the learner). The less the curriculum engages the learner's experience and culture, the less likely it is to make the connections. The more a teacher discusses going home to parents who love you with students who are orphans, or who are abused, or who are being raised by grandparents or other nonparents, the less connections will be found. Multiply the example of connections within the Des Moines, Iowa, classroom for a new immigrant from Pakistan or a typical suburban literature course for a rap-oriented urban child.

A century ago philosopher John Dewey (1916) argued in *Democracy and Education* that schools typically dried out the learning environment, leaving it dusty and brittle. He wanted education to be lively, like the children who, too often, it sedated. He intuitively imagined a synergy between the experience of living and more formal, organized education, thinking that schools, rightly built and used, could build off the lived experience of each child to simultaneously teach content, skill, and values. As a philosopher, he was recording his observations and beliefs. Now, we can confirm Dewey's observations with research findings and use our new knowledge and capacity to create such learning models.

Service-Learning at Monterey Bay

Since our founding, California State University–Monterey Bay has tried to harness the value of this synergy as an organizational and educational strategy. As one example, we require two semesters of service-learning before graduation. With this program, we have redefined the teaching and learning experience to include the communities around us, supported by technology and an outcomes-based curriculum. Collectively, these several features (community resources and internship, technology, outcomes-based education, university seminar, and the diversity of our students and the community) give us an educational outcome that is greater than the sum of its parts.

For our students, the first experience in service-learning is organized as a general, cross-cultural learning experience with people and in situations different from the one in which they grew up. It includes reading, writing, group discussions, and sponsored experiential learning in a community setting. It is designed to create real, lived experience with people, traditions, and beliefs other than your own and, by making the foreign more familiar, to deepen your potential for learning. It's a way to organize learning about a world broader than the one we've previously experienced.

Shortly after we initiated the service-learning program, a student stopped me near my office. "Dr. Smith," he said brimming with excitement, "now I understand that Charles Dickens isn't just an author and *Oliver Twist* is more than just another book." It was a bit of an odd beginning to a conversation, I thought, but I said I was glad for his learning and said so.

"No, no, you don't understand." He persisted. He told me that, for service-learning, he'd gone to work at Dorothy's Kitchen, a food shelter for the homeless in Salinas. "All these homeless kids are there, you know? I mean, every day. They're . . . they're, well, you can't help but care about them." He was becoming emotional. "You know how Dickens wrote about all that stuff, about how factories in the industrial revolution gave us progress but also ruined lots of stuff, you know . . . so Oliver and the other kids learned to be pickpockets just to live, you know?" I said I knew. "Well," he said, quieter, "at Dorothy's there are all these homeless kids just like Oliver. I don't know why I never saw them before, but I didn't. And now that I see them every day, all of a sudden I see everything differently here in Monterey County."

I went home that night and told Sally that something good was happening on campus because something important was happening in the community. Learning was happening.

For this young man, good literature had become a source of organizing experience into knowledge. His mind had taken in Dickens's depictions of the ravages of industrial revolution. Now, at Dorothy's Kitchen, he was looking into the human face of hunger and homelessness. When he lifted a child and felt her rib cage through a threadbare dress, he was holding a new understanding in his hands. He was learning. And, in his learning, he was being opened to the peculiarly American value of service to the community. For one student, a concept had become flesh and bone, and his college experience had become part of a larger learning society.

Our service-learning requirement for juniors and seniors asks each learner to apply the knowledge of his or her academic major to a significant community problem. It allows us, together, to find a connection between the core academic interest of the learner and the needs of the community. Why? Because such learning is deep and lasting; it enables students to experience civic engagement in a way that may persuade them to value it in the future.

But it isn't cheap and it isn't easy. Cal State–Monterey Bay invests heavily in service-learning because we believe it adds significant educational value to our students' lives. By making it a general education and a major requirement for graduation, we have integrated it into the heart of our academic and economic model. We allocate college work-study money to student leaders who are trained and work in the program, University Service Advocates. And our technology allows us to communicate among students, faculty, and placement agencies in the field continuously and effectively, identifying problems and cutting heavily into the otherwise exorbitant travel/supervisory costs that would be associated with having thousands of students a year in the field.

Understanding the Emerging Learning Ethos

Higher education has the knowledge and capacity at hand to develop and adopt a new mindset about what an education is and how we organize to support it. It will require a different lexicon, a new structure, a significantly different arrangement of partners and alliances. This new mindset includes an emerging set of core values about teaching and learning. Some of them are:

Life is the source and repository of learning. A printed syllabus is not. There must be a connection between the learner's experience and the material being learned.

The community harbors vast learning resources and opportunities. We learn best in communities, not outside of them. The new learning ethos will use workplaces, libraries, museums, and personal experiences as the laboratories for significant learning. And the human resources of the community, including its cultural traditions, will become teaching and learning resources.

Most learners can be successful, and the learner's success is our responsibility. In too many cases, when learners fail, educators have failed. With better diagnosis of the learner's profile, curricula can be organized and taught to promote high levels of learning and success.

College is a bridge to opportunity, not a device to weed out people. It is our job, with others, to close the opportunity gap between groups of Americans.

Diversity is an educational asset to be mined, not a problem to be masked. Diversity—of race, gender, cultural tradition, learning style, or ethnicity—is not a rough edge to be smoothed or a weakness to be remediated. We need college graduates who are confident in their own cultural identity and who can communicate across cultural differences and work with customers or teammates to solve community or corporate problems. Diversity is a source of new learning, new opportunities, and new strengths to be introduced in the curriculum.

Quality is defined by outcomes in the life of the learner. Quality is not defined by inputs called "teaching." We now have the opportunity to publicly say what we want our graduates to be able to do and then provide information that indicates how well we, and they, did in achieving those objectives. Significantly, the focus is changing from the inputs to the results.

Great teaching is greatly needed. And, although it may look different and present differently, great teaching will be more important than ever. When married to available technology, it will not necessarily be time- or place-based, or limited to a single cultural model or tradition.

The idea of the campus as the teaching center is being replaced by the idea of the community as a learning center. This single change of perspective points us in a new direction. It evokes the right questions, such as: In a learning society, what's the role of a college? How do we contribute to what our society wants? Just as online reservation services have challenged the travel agencies, e-cards have bedeviled Hallmark, and the web has driven music publishers mad; our ability to learn anything, anywhere, anytime shifts the balance of power away from the traditional model of universities and into the communities that surround them.

Jean Piaget's research on the development of cognitive capacity further suggests how seriously flawed the traditional approach to student learning is. Piaget demonstrated that as a child's brain grows through puberty, much of the learning is "additive" (one block of knowledge is stacked on another). Beyond puberty, however, our learning is increasingly "adaptive," meaning we evaluate what we are told based on our experience. And Tough's research tells us that we are constantly learning, even if our learning is never analyzed and assigned a value by a college.

We know that intelligence has several faces. Building on earlier work, Dr. Howard Gardner (1983) has identified and described several different ways that we, as individuals, use intelligence to experience and understand the world around us. The artist and the mathematician see and experience the world differently. The introvert and the extrovert work differently. The naturalist and the athlete react instinctively differently to phenomena around them.

We know that every human being has a personal learning portrait that is as distinct from others as a Monet from a Picasso, or a comic cartoon from a high-rise's blueprint. And we know that a doctor would not dream of prescribing medication or recommending treatment without taking the time to learn important diagnostic information about the person in front of her. But in higher education, where we now have the capacity to do the same kind of diagnosis with every learner, we typically look the other way and do this year what we did last. We are guilty of being more tuition-friendly than learning-friendly. And it is the students who suffer.

Colleges and universities could organize themselves in ways that harness and direct the energy of natural learning, converting it to more formal learning by connecting a known curriculum directly to the lives of learners. Just as surfers use the natural energy of the wave for their ride, educators can use the natural energy of the instinct to learn to organize educational programs. We can revise the basic architecture, staffing, financing, and governance of schools based on how learning actually occurs. Or we can continue as we have, ignoring what is known and hoping that students will make the necessary connections on a random and haphazard basis so that learning will occur.

When universities fail students, the rationalization is, "They weren't ready for college." In fact, in too many cases, college was not ready for them.

Personal learning, lying within our lived experience, is the platform on which all other learning is built. We learn more by actively and intuitively comparing our own experience to the information being presented and reflecting on the differences and similarities. This means that we will not be able to learn as effectively without an active, understood awareness of our lived experience.

At California State University–Monterey Bay we have begun to work at linking the power of the natural learning cycle with the formal learning that students do. We acknowledge that the entire university experience, as well as each course, are learning projects as Tough has described them. And we know that each learner brings a unique combination of experience and intelligence to the effort.

Using a class called the ProSeminar, we now ask our learners to probe—for themselves, but also for us—why they are at college, what they want from the experience, and what learning plan we can develop together to support their aspirations.

We ask our students to think about the consequences of their learning, where they want to be on their journey when they finish our section of the trail. We want them to develop their own expectations for learning, and to be willing to share those expectations with us so that we can effectively be educators. Our curriculum begins not with answers but with questions, asking our learners to engage, to employ what they are learning in some practical way and then to reflect on what they have done and learned.

Engagement creates the raw material for learning. And the learning derives from the lived experience for each learner. Then, active reflection, considering what you have done, what you have learned, and how you are different as a result, converts the raw material of experience to learning and knowledge for each learner, as it does for all of us, everywhere, at every stage of life. It's in this learning cycle that students discover meaning, connecting their experience and the learning it contains to their own hearts and aspirations.

We believe that if we want to educate people to be learners throughout their lives, we must help them develop and practice the intellectual characteristics that underlie learning. And we believe that it is critically important to identify through practice and research how technology can enhance the teaching and learning process. The

Visible Knowledge Project (http://crossroads.georgetown.edu/vkp/) is a national effort based at Georgetown University to link interactive technology, active research, and learning. Our participating faculty structure their curricula to make explicit their learning objectives, student learning outcomes, the values inherent in the curriculum, and the intellectual capacities that they are trying to teach. Our outcomes-based academic model supports this approach to teaching and learning. And, because we also employing Dr. Ernest Boyer's scholarship of teaching and learning, the faculty are simultaneously modeling high-level professional behavior by integrating active research on teaching and learning with their classes while engaging students in the process.

Our participating faculty do this not simply for their satisfaction and improvement, but also for the students'; and not simply for the term of their college education, but for the life that follows it. By being conscious about their own learning in college, students are learning how to learn later on in their careers, their families, and their communities. It is how they will become and remain outstanding engineers in their careers, and it is also how they will be informed, thoughtful citizens in the voting booth. They will know how to keep learning in conscious and reflective ways long after the campus lights have been turned off.

My grandfather believed that either you were smart or you were not. He was a wonderful man. But on this score, he was wrong. Like him, however, most of us in education have treated intelligence as if it were a commodity and not a capacity. Now we know, thanks to Howard Gardner's groundbreaking research, that intelligence is a tool for learning, an inherent way of experiencing the world. Gardner has identified more than nine different intelligences that learners use to make meaning from the world around them, much as a potter can use different clays and mixtures to make art. Where Allen Tough described how people go about learning, Howard Gardner described the different ways people use intelligence to learn. His research taught us, as educators, to recognize that intelligence has different forms and, employed thoughtfully, can be a personal tool for deeper and more effective learning. Not everyone will learn in the same way. In this recognition—that individuals learn differently—the pedagogical ax is put to the root of any education, including higher education, that says one-size-fits-all in the classroom.

Conclusion: Employing the New Ethos

We know right now how to fit many sizes as the new learning ethos develops. Influenced by the ethos, many of today's learners will not care as much about traditions of research and knowledge creation. Neither will they equate the value of a degree with the length of time spent studying on a campus. What's being requested is learning that meets a learner's objectives and develops intellectual, social, civic, and economic capacities that are valued in the marketplace and society. For example, Alverno College, a small private college in Milwaukee, has reinvented itself over the last 30 years as one of America's premier outcome-based learning institutions. At Alverno, you proceed to graduation based on the learning results you can demonstrate. And the record compiled by Alverno's graduates, in the workforce and graduate school, is as strong as its ability to retain and graduate the students it admits.

We also know that, through experience and personal learning, people learn continuously and they learn differently. We know that learners constantly adapt their learning to the circumstances and the needs of their personal situation. Therefore, we can conclude that if a school wants to be learner focused, it must begin by learning itself: Who are these individuals that are coming to us? What are their needs and goals? How does each of them learn best? We need to ask the right questions before we rush off to apply the splint. And when we do, we will begin to connect the lived experience of every person with his formal education. When natural learning and formal learning are joined, each will become more powerful, more useful, and more successful in the life of the learner.

5

▼

PERSONAL LEARNING,
REFLECTION, AND GROWTH

Recall the idyllic image of ivy-covered campuses where professors share obtuse humor, students haunt musty libraries, and male trustees gather for after-dinner conversation with brandy and cigars at the local country club. Now imagine that down the sidewalk outside that country club roar three skateboarders, baseball caps backwards and sideways, headphones blasting rap music into their ears. They ride down handrails designed for the elderly; they leap curbs, landing just beyond precious shrubs. They fall down and get up, bruised, careening out of sight behind the gardener's shed. Meet the actual learning society where change is the constant, where opportunity has a different face and plays to a different beat, where all learning is personal. Our ability to learn continuously and purposefully throughout our lives will determine our ability to grow and prosper. We have come into an age in which learning is the most critical survival skill.

If we look back on our collegiate experiences from the viewpoint of, say, our 50th birthday, it becomes clear that college has accounted for a miniscule part of all that we have learned. We learn:

- When we read about child development and discuss parenting with a friend or in an organized group in order to cope better with the children in our lives; and when
- Our supervisor at work asks us to help solve a problem facing the company, demonstrates a new technique, brings in a lecturer to describe a new development in the industry; and when
- We develop a health and diet plan to keep physically fit while eating well; and when
- We read several books on China or Mexico to know more about those countries or to plan a trip; and when
- We study investment practices and then practice with our investments in order to make more with the small amount we have laid aside; and when
- We discuss and read about soils and seeds prior to starting our first serious garden; and when
- We learn to cope, live alone, and create a new future after a divorce or a loss through death; and when
- We learn to play an instrument or a new sport, or engage in therapy. (Smith, 1986, pp. 19–20)

As a professional educator, one of my first and most formative learning projects was founding the Community College of Vermont in 1970. As described earlier, we designed the college's innovative learning systems and implemented them across Vermont between 1970 and 1978. I was 25 years old when we began. I'd never managed anything substantial. I'd certainly never founded a college. I now suspect that I had not yet learned enough to know that we should not succeed in what we were doing. One observer characterized our entire operation as the "bumblebee college" because although the laws of physics suggest that bumblebees are too heavy to fly, they do. He thought that our operation, both educationally and politically, defied gravity.

Sometime during those early years I was described by one of my close friends and colleagues in an article he wrote.

> Smith, a consummate politician, capable of resolving conflicts with dazzling skill, found it difficult to draw lines clearly enough to form a coherent basis for action. His genius lay in the ability to blur distinctions, make new connections, create novel relationships. (Daloz, 1982)

Forgiving the hyperbole in his quote, what I realize today is that what someone else characterized as genius was simply using my instinct. I was unaware of what I knew and didn't know, what I was doing and not doing. I was like the man going through a forest without a compass; I kept walking, doing my best, hoping for a good outcome, assuming I would emerge but not knowing exactly where.

At the same time, I was neither an accomplished manager nor a planner. I had some skills, but only some. I possessed a bit of vision, but not enough. I knew I couldn't create the college alone. Thus, earlier learning projects had provided a hugely necessary lesson. As the same writer cited above said, describing my relationship with the college's planner, during the same period of time.

> . . . while he [Smith] would have had to agree that he had no idea what to do with a planner, he knew also that he did need what Steve [Hochschild] promised: a systematic, rational approach to management. This tension was to characterize the relationship between the two men as long as they worked together . . . In a way, it was a unique combination of artist and critic. And, for several years, it worked remarkably well. (Daloz, 1982)

In retrospect, our collective effort was successful enough to survive and go on to greater heights. Today, it prospers.

But the college's endurance and success also have their roots in the decision I made to leave the presidency in 1978. I chose to leave because, after eight years in the presidency, what I did not know was catching up with me. I was capable of launching an innovative college but not, I was learning on the job, of serving as its continuing leader. I realized with some pain that I had worked myself beyond my level of competence, that the job increasingly called for more than I knew. That meant that the longer I stayed, the less effective I would become. So, I faced a choice. Either leave soon, hoping to be remembered kindly as a founding visionary, or tough it out and be removed in a less attractive fashion in a year or two. I made the difficult personal decision to leave this extraordinary career opportunity behind. I chose to resign and look for the next challenge. It was a turning point in my life.

Whether my eight years in the president's chair was one learning project or a collection of learning projects is not immediately important. But it is clear that learning first equipped me and that more learning ultimately warned me.

In the years after leaving, I finished my doctoral studies, using them to try to understand why the educational and organizational models employed in the development of the Community College of Vermont had succeeded. Importantly, my graduate school admitted me as a special student who, with advisor, was permitted to follow his own learning objectives as opposed to the established curriculum with prerequisite requirements. During that time, using classes, independent study, and a lot of reflection, I learned why the college had been successful educationally and why my intuitive sense that if I had stayed, I would have failed, was right. Out of the raw material of that experience, with reflection, I learned. I began to understand my strengths and my weaknesses as a leader. In the end, I was powerfully reminded that we succeeded because we were a team with a shared vision and diverse, mutually compensating sets of values, skills, and perspectives.

Many traditional colleges, as centers of teaching rather than communities of learning, do not allow the kind of exploration that my graduate school did. Nor do they grant credit for learning done outside of the course structure. At the Community College of Vermont, however, we believed that if you already knew something, you did not need to learn it again. If you already knew something required for graduation, and you could document it, you should get credit for it. It seemed like common sense. Thus, we offered a seminar in which students organized and documented their experiential learning in portfolios that were assessed for credit. It was a reasonable way to reduce redundancy, save time and money, and help our adult students reach their objectives more efficiently and effectively.

Recognition of a student's knowledge rewards the student's learning (the outcome) rather than the traditional college experience (the process). For colleges to admit and teach learners, especially older learners, without assessing their prior experiential learning and developing a learning profile that assesses and describes the contours of her learning styles and multiple intelligences, is tantamount to doctors not doing a standard workup on every patient that comes to them.

On a sunny summer day in 1973 the Community College of Vermont held its first graduation on the steps of the state capitol in Montpelier, Vermont. Our graduates' achievement marked a huge milestone, symbolic and substantive, for them as well as for the college. Dignitaries, family members, and graduates milled around.

After the ceremony, one of the graduates, Nancy, approached me. A fortyish, practical woman, Nancy ran a nearby childcare center and had enrolled to get a degree combining child development and management. Her degree work had involved a great deal of assessment and validation as well as some course work. Much of what we had done was to allow Nancy, in an assessment seminar, to collect and organize her documentation so experts and professors in the field could review it and assign appropriate credit. After she'd received a transcript showing the credit value of her previous learning, she was within reach of her degree.

Nancy was older than I, and in some ways she was wiser. "Peter," she said as we walked down the capitol's steps, "thank you for the degree. It's what I came for. But it's not the most important thing that I learned. Thank you for helping me to understand that I am a learner, that I learn all the time. Thanks for respecting my learning with your assessments."

Nancy was making three points. She acknowledged the importance of the degree. Second, she had realized that our acknowledgment of her previous learning was a validation of her; it was respectful and fair. But the third element of her message was news to me, big news. The assessment process itself, with the reflection it required, was deeply educational. It had enabled Nancy to see she had been a learner her entire life and to understand her experiential learning from an arm's length view. Now she had the intellectual tools to consciously continue what she had been doing reflexively before: to be a learner, now a more conscious learner, who meets each new challenge and opportunity with growth.

Remember the Scarecrow in *The Wizard of Oz?* He had shown great ingenuity and intelligence throughout his travels with Dorothy, but he believed that he knew nothing, that he had no brain. Ultimately, the Wizard knew what to do.

"Can't you give me brains?" asked the Scarecrow.

"You don't need them. You are learning something every day. A baby has brains, but it doesn't know much. Experience is the only thing that brings knowledge, and the longer you are on earth, the more experience you are sure to get."

"That may all be true," said the Scarecrow, "but I shall be unhappy unless you give me brains."

The false Wizard looked at him carefully, "You don't need brains, you need confidence. Back where I come from, we have universities, seats of great learning, where men go to become great thinkers. And when they come out they think deep thoughts, and with no more brains than you have. But they have one thing you haven't got, a diploma. Therefore, by virtue of the authority vested in me by the Universitatus Comitatus E Pluribus Unum, I hereby confer upon you the Honorary Degree of Th.D.—Doctor of Thinkology . . . "

"Oh!" said the Scarecrow. "The sum of the square roots of any two sides of an isosceles triangle is equal to the square root of the remaining side . . . Oh joy! Oh rapture! I've got a brain." (Smith, 1986, p. 15)

If collegiate leaders would be annoyed by the comparison of this whimsy to their serious task, it is understandable. But the comparison is inescapable. We tend, in the classic collegiate model, to treat incoming students like a mass of people without brains. We stuff them all into the same curriculum by the thousand. We plunk them down in massive lecture halls to have wisdom dispensed and received. Eventually we confer on them a degree and they send their mortarboards soaring. "Oh joy! Oh rapture! We have our degrees!"

More seriously, beyond the campus lies the community populated by men and women of all ages and conditions who lack a degree, an enormous wasted human resource to our economy and our society. Whatever their station in life, they have this in common: The establishment has never confirmed their learning. Thus, like penniless children pressing noses against the candy store window, personal learners are left on the outside, sensing their capacity but unable to reach the credentials and rewards that colleges have to offer.

Because collegiate degrees carry with them both real and symbolic power, it's imperative that we find ways in this learning age to get such degrees to the highest number of qualified people possible. There is a cost, both to the individual and the larger society, in the opportunity lost because of our unwillingness to harness the knowledge and experience that personal learners already have. We need to embrace and authenticate learning regardless of where it has occurred, not pretend that such learning is inferior because it was secured without our aid. It is hubris, or worse, that allows American colleges and universities to tell incoming students—especially older, so-called nontraditional students—that the learning they possess should have no impact on the learning they must still achieve.

The Role of Experience
Personal learning is the way we breathe in new ideas, new behaviors, and new knowledge and live beyond the old. It acts as our internal

gyroscope creating balance out of imbalance and allowing us to adapt and cope to new situations, demands, and opportunities. Such learning may be pleasant or unpleasant, difficult or easy, but it is not incidental. It is not frosting; it's the cake.

Every time we complete a learning project, we have gone through four stages: assessment, planning, implementation, and evaluation. We can imagine them as four arcs that form one circle of a constantly ascending spiral. We come around the circle, mastering new learning, only to start into the next circle to find new knowledge. The four stages can also be construed as answers to these four questions: Where am I? Where do I want to go? How am I going to get there? How will I know when I've arrived?

Personal learning allows us to learn in whatever way we learn best. Too often, in a college setting, we are forced to learn in the traditional academic mode: sitting and listening, taking notes, and trying to remember and recall. But Gardner's research on multiple intelligences, described earlier, tells us that we each have a distinctive way of interpreting the world. Unlike our experience with most schooling, personal learning allows us, instead of living in someone else's straight jacket, to move more freely on our own. The first step is to make sure that each person becomes conscious and deliberate about her or his personal learning. By knowing how we learn, by learning the importance of reflection, we can make conscious learning a lifelong process.

The Value of Reflection

But there's a problem with our learning projects. Allen Tough's research revealed that most people had forgotten the learning projects they had undertaken until he dredged it up through memory exercises. In other words, we tend to forget not only that we learned, but also what we learned. It's true of most of us. We are continuously learning and changing, but we don't realize it.

Gail Sheehy's *Passages* (1976) taught many of us about the transitions of age and development through which we move. As I read the book, I was struck by how often the passage in question was voiced as a negative event in life. I questioned myself then, "Are all developmental passages negative?" Some calls to reflection are gentle: We go on vacation and read a book we've meant to read for years; somehow, in the reading of it, we hear the call to introspection and change. Some calls are brutal: Our child dashes into the traffic and cannot be brought back to life; our loving mother is strangled by Alzheimer's before our eyes; we are called into our supervisor's office for coffee and told we are out of work. What evokes the call to reflect varies widely not only between individuals but even within each of our lives. But once the reflection begins, it proceeds with a purpose.

I remember a day in the late 1980s when Sally and I were sorting old photographs. It was one of those lazy Sunday afternoon jobs for a winter weekend. I came across a picture of me cradling one of our sons. It had been taken a dozen years earlier during my final days at the Community College of Vermont. As I looked at my smiling face in the photo, I realized with a physical shock that I was looking at a stranger, a person who no longer existed. This wasn't the face I saw in the mirror as I shaved each morning. This was someone young, insulated by his own naiveté, mostly unscarred and unseasoned. I wasn't that person any longer!

The intervening 12 years had rushed by: elections won and lost, a business venture, success on a school board, my father's and mother-in-law's deaths, becoming a father a third time. It was dizzying. There was a chasm of unreflected experience between the man in the picture and the person I had become. Looking at the stranger in that photograph, I realized that a river of unreflected learning and change had flowed by and over me. For whatever reasons—and there were many at play that Sunday afternoon, some glaringly public and others intensely personal—the shock of seeing myself other than I was demanded my attention. I realized I had grown away from the earlier version and become, for better or for worse, a new and different person (Smith, 1986). On that Sunday afternoon I began developing "Smith's theory of reflection."

Webster's dictionary says reflection is the act of "careful consideration and the results thereof." Rita Weathersby, a developmental theorist, claims it is how we make meaning from experience. I'm happy to draw on both definitions, thinking of reflection as the act or means by which we convert information and the raw material of experience into knowledge. When we reflect on what we know and what we've experienced, we gain control of our lives, developing an understanding of what is happening and who we are becoming and why. When we do not reflect in this way, we are eventually flying without any personal radar, risking the living of our lives as victims of circumstance and prisoners of our own experience and learning.

The theory holds that there are times in a person's life when he updates his personally held image and understanding of who he is. That image, that person, is the person you see in the mirror every morning. But after the update, life continues, giving you new experiences and new learning, which as it accumulates, goes largely unnoticed and unreflected. So, gradually yet ineluctably, you change, literally growing away from the person you were when you last took stock because of the experience you are accumulating and its cumulative impact on you. In this progression of events, there comes a moment when the new you, the becoming you, outweighs the older image, creating confusion and imbalance in your life. Then, almost always due to an external triggering event, you are forced into a crisis of rediscovery through reflection.

The phrase "learning projects" sounds neat and nicely organized, well packaged. In fact, our adult experience with learning projects is ordinarily anything but tidy. We learn as we live, lurching from one thing to another, rarely achieving our goals on first attempts, learning as we go. Sometimes we learn as a way of coping with personal crises and changing. So, often, our most significant learning comes at untidy times in our lives. In addition to the untidiness, however, most of us haven't learned how to reflect consciously and seriously on the fact of our personal learning, let alone its value and impact on us. So, in many cases, learning is lodged in our lives as an iceberg of experience revealing tips of knowledge. But through active reflection we can convert the raw material of experience to the more refined distillate of knowledge, achieving a finer alignment between our lived experience and our conscious knowledge. Imagine a college that helped learners develop that ability.

Personal Assessment

As we learn, we change. Whether or not we are aware of our own learning, at some point we all recognize that we have changed. Understanding personal learning depends on recognizing its larger, often hidden meaning and placing a value on it. Our learning matters to us: We will measure it, appreciate it, supplement it. We'll see the gaps and areas needing improvement. We will set our own, new goals. Thus, we will be engaged in the process of assessment. We will see how what we've learned affects, and is affected by, what we've experienced. We will become, as learners, more self-aware, masters of our experience, no longer dependent on others to tell us what and when and how to learn.

Consider the case of Elaine McDermott. Elaine was our neighbor in Vermont. She had been a math teacher before she raised her two daughters. And she had always planned to go back to teaching when her daughters were in school. But when actually confronted with her version of the stranger in her mirror, Elaine set out on a very different path.

For years I had been thinking that when the girls were in school, I would go back to teaching.

The first year I took a temporary job at a local company running their retail store. I was planning to apply for teaching jobs the following fall. My whole attitude about running the store was that this was fun. I kept telling people that I was just doing it for now, until I could get a job teaching, because I wasn't growing, I wasn't learning anything. I felt I had control over it.

Then they took it all away from me on New Year's Eve. There had been two major layoffs before then so the handwriting was on the wall. But I thought that I still had a couple of months if it was their choice, and if it was mine, I had until June.

I was in a sort of state of shock for three weeks. It sounds like a strong statement, but I think I was because as I look back on it, I couldn't identify what was going on at the time. I was staying home saying, "Isn't this just wonderful, I can spend all day reading." But it was awful and I couldn't recognize that. After about a month, I realized, "My god, what am I going to do? My kids are in school, and I'm thirty-five years old, and I've got to get my act together."

I had a friend who was going through a divorce—not by her choice. She was the victim and she went through what happens to a lot of women who follow their husbands around as a career and haven't established anything for themselves. I thought that if I didn't find something, if I didn't get my act together, I could be the same woman.

So I said, "Okay, you can't wait until June any more. Now what are you going to do?" Well I was going to teach because that had been my pat answer for the past ten years. So, I started to send resumes to different schools. Then I started getting replies. That was the thing that threw me into a depression, because, at that point I had to make a commitment. Writing the letters was no commitment.

I didn't want to teach anymore. It was just something that I hadn't thought about for ten years. I always thought that's what I would do when the kids were grown. But I heard George on the phone one day, telling his parents that I was going to teach, and hearing it like a third party. All of a sudden I said, "Wait a minute. That's not me. I don't think I'm going to do that. No. I'm not going to do that." (Smith, 1986, pp. 24–27)

During those years at home, Elaine's life changed outwardly. But she wasn't aware of a concurrent inner change until she was forced into reflection after being laid off. It was not always easy and quiet; it was, in fact, hard and disquieting. But it left Elaine with a sharper awareness of her values and dreams. Despite the thousands of times she had affirmed it, she did not want to go back to teaching. And it took a period and process of reflection to yield the self-awareness she needed.

I had always been interested in the law. At one point, I had regretted that I hadn't done something in the law when I got out of college. I had heard of the school before, but I just kind of filed it. Every now and then I'd bring it up with people when I still thought I had a choice. But it was just part of something I was faintly considering.

It was just not knowing what I was going to do. There was an orientation meeting the following Thursday night. I thought, "Maybe that's what I need right now." So, I gave them a call and told them I'd be there.

That unlocked something. It cemented the decision and my resolve to go. I felt as if I had made a commitment to do something that had been in me for a long time. I sat down that day and wrote two letters, one to my in-laws and one to a friend, and I told them that I was going to paralegal school. (pp. 24–27)

All the ingredients of learning were necessary for Elaine: information, experience, and reflection. Her courage and persistence enabled her to make use of what some would have regarded as a midlife crisis, and borrowing again from Allen Tough, converting it into a marvelous learning project.

Personal learning changes the learner. But if the change is unrecognized and unplanned, unaccounted for, unacknowledged, then we can become strangers to ourselves, prisoners of our experience. If we fail to reflect on and learn from our individual learning, we can become lost, wandering through our lives, controlled by our experience's impact on us but unable to benefit from what they have taught us.

In an earlier and simpler era, the instinct to learn was a major dynamic in an otherwise stable setting. We had time to figure things out in their own good time. That's no longer true. Today we must be able to achieve personal learning within professional and other environments that are changing rapidly, profoundly. It's like a carnival ride with two sections spinning in different directions simultaneously, personal learning whirling one direction within a larger, swirling vortex of societal change. Everything is moving at one time. Reflection must be done on the run. Where personal learning used to occur in a stable and predictable environment, it has become yet another element of change in a world characterized by change.

At the heart of the emerging learning ethos is the capability to turn the potential crisis of experience without reflection into the soft landing of personal learning through reflection. All learning, personal and formal, is connected to the lived experience. As my mentor and friend, Harvey Scribner, Vermont's former commissioner of education, would remind me, "You must remember, Peter, that the word 'education' is descended from the Latin *ex ducare* meaning 'to lead from, or to lead beyond.' Education is not a journey of teaching; it is a journey of learning."

Consider Peg Moore's journey. I met Peg Moore in 1982. She had become the director of her local public health center in Boston without a traditional education, and I was interested in knowing how it had happened. Peg's journey was a little more conscious and planned. But her personal learning, stubbornness, and good fortune in ultimately finding a university that would assess her experiential learning ultimately gave her the traction to continue.

Like all my friends, I went to work after high school and loved working. I met my husband and we got married about a year later. I got pregnant right away and had my first child two weeks before I turned twenty. My second child was born about a year later, and the third a few years after that.

I worked at a bank from when I was a junior to just before I got married. After that, I worked at a theatrical agency as a bookkeeper until my pregnancy would not allow me to work any longer outside of the house. Money was very tight so I had to find bookkeeping work at home so I could take care of my babies and bring in some money.

When I had my third child, I was still working at home. I became very interested in the health care of the North End community because two of my children were asthmatics. I found it extremely difficult to get help for them. One day, I heard there was a meeting in the community around health care issues, so I went to it. I got very interested in trying to get better health care here, and began to go to those meetings regularly.

Eventually, the group asked me to chair those meetings. I knew absolutely nothing about chairing a meeting. I didn't know protocol and I still don't. But I did it. After working over a year, we were able to open the doors of this health care facility and begin providing services here in the North End.

In 1972, the board asked me to take on the job as director of the center. I was very uncomfortable with that because I was concerned that I wouldn't do the community just service because I didn't have an education. But I knew what the community would accept and what they would not. I also knew my limitations and wasn't afraid to ask for help. Also, when I was chair of the board, we had a consultant doing a lot of the legwork. He kept me abreast of what was going on so that I was doing some of the actual work from day one also. I worked in every aspect of the center's development including construction.

So, reluctantly, I decided to take on the role with the help of some friends in the health care field. They said they'd tell me to get out if I wasn't doing a just service to community by holding this job without a degree . . . if that was a hindrance to the health center.

I've changed a lot over the years since I took this job. I used to be very much in awe of people. If someone were a doctor or a lawyer or a teacher, it was like, "Oh my God, they're better than I am." There are a lot of people who are like me when it comes to dealing with professional people. Working in this job, I found that everyone was a human being. You put your pants on the same way as the other guy. I had to stop being in awe of people and begin to feel as if I were on the same level so that I could be successful at what I was trying to do. As a result, my negotiating skills became a lot stronger. I know that I learn something everyday. I know that I've learned something when I can take it and apply it to something else. Then I've learned it.

Now I'm going to learn a whole new area—nursing home care. Some of it I'll apply to my knowledge from here and there, personnel policies, dealing with people, third party reimbursements. But, there are other components of nursing home care where I have no knowledge so I'm looking forward to learning them.

The sad part is that the degree—that piece of paper—is very meaningful to other people. It was really frowned on when I would send a proposal into a government agency and they would ask what my background was. I graduated from high school. Period. I mean it was like, "What? You don't have a master's degree?" They were thinking, "What do you have, a Mickey Mouse operation going on there?"

You just can't seem to get your foot inside the door without the degree. I know a man who works in an insurance company. He has all kinds of certificates from school programs and conferences and things that he's done in the insurance business. But when an opening occurred elsewhere in the building, he applied and they said, "Well, you don't have the degree." They would take someone with a degree in gardening because they had the piece of paper and bypass the person who has the experience in the area where they're looking. It happens all the time. It's very frustrating. (Smith, 1986, pp. 55–59)

Peg Moore identified her personal learning and used it to survive what otherwise loomed as a crisis. She may be surprised at the things she has achieved and the impact her learning has had on her. But she developed new attitudes and learned new skills that bolstered her capacity to lead and serve. As with the learning most of us achieve, hers seemed unexceptional to her when taken piece by piece. But its collective impact was significant.

Personal learning stimulates change. It also equips us to survive change. If, as Allen Tough has found, most people learn continually, then recognizing our learning is the first step toward taking control over it and adding purposefully to it. It is one thing to recognize your personal learning. But it is quite another to be denied the academic, social, economic and community value of such learning. How would you feel if you recognized your personal learning only to find that the community's leaders didn't care, that your learning would have no impact on your degrees, your employment, your wages, or your community status? If you can imagine that, then you can imagine why Peg Moore was haunted by her lack of a college degree. It wasn't that she lacked learning; like the Scarecrow, she lacked a degree.

Conclusion: Personal Learning Needs Formal Recognition

On the one hand it is true that learning limited to classrooms will no longer suffice. In this sense, graduation is no longer a meaningful dividing line between the time when we learn and the time when we are done learning. But, on the other hand, simply recognizing the value of our personal learning is not enough either. It's a nice ideal, but does not deliver the value we need. We need to remember Margery Moore's admonition. Personal learning needs to be formally recognized, and learning projects, the natural pattern by which we all learn, need to be used as the basis for college credit that leads to degrees. It is what we have learned over the last 30 years that compels us to redefine the personal, economic, and social value of personal learning through reflection.

This new knowledge about how people learn enriches the mix of diversity issues in education. Now, if we want all learners to have a solid shot at success, we must also consider their diversity of life experience and learning, their learning style, and intelligence profile, as well as ethnic and cultural traditions.

6

▼

DIVERSITY: THE TIE THAT BINDS

I wonder what Senator J. William Fulbright would say if he could see America today.

He was a remarkable man, creator in 1946 of the prestigious Fulbright scholarships that ushered in a new era of international education and cross-cultural learning long before such things were popular. In the early years of the age of mass destruction after America had used the atomic bomb, in the face of rising isolationism in America, Fulbright saw international education as a key to national security. He reasoned that if enough people experienced cultures other than their own, the prospects for mutual destruction would wane in the face of the shared experience of increasing understanding, knowledge, mutual respect, and friendship. His was a simple and profound concept that has proven itself through wonderful results over the years.

Fulbright once explained his mission this way:

> Our future is not in the stars but in our minds and hearts. Creative leadership and liberal education, which in fact go together, are the first requirements for a hopeful future for humankind. Fostering these—leading, learning, and empathy between cultures—was

and remains the purpose of the international scholarship program. (Fulbright, n.d.)

Today, this remains the flagship international education program
sponsored by the United States with more than 250,000 participants
including 94,000 from America and 155,600 from other countries.

Over the last 60 years, however, we have come face-to-face with a
new national security problem that lives right here at home. Instead of
mutually assured nuclear destruction internationally, we have a growing
domestic challenge marked by widening gaps among our own citizens
characterized by ethnic background, gender preference, learning styles
and intelligence, education attainment, and income levels. Our need
for increased understanding, knowledge, friendship, and mutual respect
lies right here at home as well as beyond our borders. And, other than
Fulbright's advice on creative leadership and liberal education, we have
no effective antidotes to the social and economic decline assured by
continuing to ignore the diversity within our society that gives it its
richness and flavor.

Diversity: An Asset to Develop, Not a Deficit to Remediate

Less than 20 years after the Fulbright scholarships were established,
Michael Harrington (1962) wrote his classic, *The Other America*.
Harrington put a human face on the grinding poverty in our cities and
countryside. *The Other America* was a mirror in which all Americans
could see ourselves. Suddenly, race and income were not simply social
or legal issues. They were human issues, worn in the faces of people
with pain, hunger, and illness looking out at us from the pages of his
book.

With his title, Harrington suggested that we have another country,
a country of greater differences and additional cultures and less income
and less education than the country we assume we are. In an age when
America was being defined by *Ozzie and Harriet* and *Leave It to Beaver,*
Harrington asserted that there was a different, less visible nation
surrounding us. We responded to *The Other America* and other forces,
including the civil rights movement, with government programs like
Volunteers in Service to America (VISTA) and the Job Corps. And

exploding media sources sensitized us to the issues of culture, ethnicity, and income. But we have continued to hold the reality of poverty at arm's length, objectifying it as someone else's problem that we needed to fix, a deficit that needed to be erased.

It has been argued that the problem with the poor is they don't have enough money. While it's hard to dispute the Yogi Berra logic here, it's also foolish to fall for it. Because if what's wrong with the poor is just a lack of cash, then a welfare check should fix poverty. We have decades of American experimentation with anti-poverty programs that have proven cash alone doesn't fix poverty. Rather, poverty, ignorance, illness, violence, and hopelessness—and, perhaps, eventually, terrorism—are the consequence of relentless, complicated, failing social systems. They have no single cause and no single solution, frustrating as this may be for Americans who love to fix what's broken.

The stakes have changed since 1965. First, we understand today that we cannot, as a nation, afford social and economic failure with millions and millions of our citizens. We know now that education is at the heart of every anti-poverty program that works: early childhood education, public education, private education, higher education, special education, lifelong education. Education is, in fact, a crusader's banner that has taken on a social and an economic as well as a moral imperative. In recent years we've come to understand more and more clearly that all people and all communities have assets that support learning. The fight for equality and opportunity in America is a fight for social survival in the learning age, and it's a fight that can be waged by communities who often have assets that those of us in power fail to recognize.

The Other America did not merely make the case about poverty and crime and social failure with tables, charts, and numbers. Harrington moved us because he offered deeply human photographs and equally compelling anecdotes. And we initiated the War on Poverty in response to what we read.

In 1989, a quarter-century after Harrington's work, the venerable American Council on Education published *Minorities on Campus: A Handbook for Enhancing Diversity*. It was, for the few that read it, a disturbing report driven by sound thinking and good people, many of them my colleagues. The title of the opening chapter told much of the story: The Issue: Lost Momentum. And the case was made in the opening four sentences:

> More than 20 years have passed since the enactment of the 1964 Civil Rights Act, and higher education has made real progress in opening up our nation's campuses to minority students. For example, in 1960 there were 150,000 black students in higher education; by 1975 that number had risen to approximately one million. But progress since then has slowed, and national commitment to equality and access seems to have faltered. Black enrollments have remained stagnant since 1975 . . . (Green, 1989, p. 1)

Recall the grim statistics. In 2000, only two-thirds of our ninth-graders graduated from high school. Less than 40% went on to college and less than 20% graduated with a degree within six years. When factored for race and income, these shocking success rates get even worse (Smith, 1986). At the same time, over 80% of the increases in college-age youth in the coming years will be in the African-American and Hispanic populations. The populations that do not prosper in our schools constitute the majority in the American future.

If we continue to have the same success rates in the future, the body count of failed learners will increase and, like a steady loss of lifeblood, their growing numbers will weaken our society. At this rate, we will "succeed" our way to societal failure. A top-end collegiate success rate of 60% after six years is unacceptably low as a national standard for everyone. It is the clearest evidence that our colleges' grading and selectivity, as well as their learning models and cultures, are shaped to reward the success of the few at the expense of growing many. Or, to paraphrase the Kansas City Monarchs' miracle man of baseball, Satchel Paige, "The hurrieder we go, the behinder we'll get."

We must succeed in bringing many more people to the table of opportunity, especially people of color and cultural difference from the mainstream Anglo population, or we risk social and economic failure as a society. Whether we are thinking of individual learners or of the American society as a whole, we must learn to bend our elbows, giving up our arm's-length approach to social, cultural and economic differences. We must learn how to greet each other's children, and each other, with the embrace of respect.

Do not misunderstand me. This is not a call to niceness. If we fail to educate across all cultural traditions to high levels of success, it won't be just a moral disappointment. It will be an economic, social, and educational curse blighting our ability to strengthen ourselves civically and compete globally. It handicaps our hopes for freedom and builds the environment for hopelessness that breeds terrorism. This isn't about niceness. It's about national priorities, national capacities, and national security.

Learning From Differences

So, what would a 21st-century Senator Fulbright propose? Fulbright knew intuitively that cultural differences and varied life experiences are untapped sources for rich learning. Today, he would look for ways to make our diversity our strength, the cultural tie that binds. Two people who've lived the same life will have less to teach each other. But two people whose life experiences have been very different bring together the energy and excitement and potential, the raw material for dynamic, enduring learning. The circumstances of individuals or families, of communities, their problems and opportunities, their faith and their wisdom, their heroes and their myths—all are assets for deep, important learning. Every one of us brings personal difference in gender, ethnic tradition, personal history, learning styles, and much more. We bring these to every learning project in life. And when we engage others with us in our learning projects, their differences enrich our own.

There is great opportunity here for improved teaching and learning, to combine our new knowledge about how people learn with the assets of diversity and the community unleashing a new synergy of rich teaching and learning. It would be, in effect, a double-winner as we simultaneously reduce the friction that results from ignoring the substance and the value of people's life experiences and learning styles while introducing those very same assets as critical elements in the learning process. If presented with these understandings, Fulbright today would instantly recognize the value of this broader definition of diversity.

For example, the lower division service-learning class at Cal State–Monterey Bay, Participating in Multicultural Communities, is one way to bring all of these disparate elements together. We purposely organize learners in groups and in seminar settings where they will be working with students from other ethnic and cultural traditions. And we also strive to place learners in community settings where they will be experiencing issues and situations different from those they are familiar with. The combined effect of the readings, the discussions, the experiences, and the company with whom each student participates in the field and in class adds up to a powerful learning experience that both validates personal history and opens the learner to others' experiences.

There is a natural synergy between the extraordinary array of diversity facing our institutions and our emerging knowledge about how people learn best. Remember the connection in Tough's (1971) research between "me," the interests and experience of the learner, and "it," the material to be learned. With the connection established and nurtured, significant learning is possible. Without it, the asset of diversity in all of its forms becomes a negative, contributing friction to the teaching-learning process, frustrating learner and teacher alike and lowering the quality of work and the achievement of the learners.

One of my teachers in this matter was Connie Yu. When I met her, she had finally become a successful commodities broker in St. Louis. But her story is packed with the emotions and experiences of many immigrants. We can hear her history in her voice as she reflects on the culture she encountered and the struggle she had to "learn" her way into it as an Asian-American woman. Her brief memoir underscores both how daunting the dominant culture of this country can be and how rich the learning can be when culture is approached as an asset.

I was born in Amoy, China, in 1936, just before the outbreak of the Second World War. When I was three, we moved to Hong Kong. During the Japanese occupation I had erratic schooling. I [eventually] went to Japanese school for a year and Chinese school for a year and when the whole thing settled down, I was in high school.

After high school, and over the objections of my parents, I became an airhostess. For three years I traveled the world as a hostess. Through traveling, I began to know that there were other cultures in this world, not just the Hong Kong culture. And I began to recognize a lack of polish in myself. Like being able to think and recognize art and literature. And to understand that the world just isn't a Jane Eyre book. There's a lot more to it than that.

When I first came to America, I really didn't like myself at all because here I am a strange creature in a country of people who all know what they're doing. And I began to realize that there were things that mattered to me that didn't seem to matter to most people around me. I was very lonely, and I had to decide either to try to reach people, to communicate, or go back where I belonged. Finally, I thought, "I'm here. This is my life. I must reach these people."

Well, first I tried to read people's minds. But how do you read people's minds without understanding what makes them feel, what makes them become what they are? There are mental thought patterns that are different—your philosophy and history. So I went back to American philosophy because I wanted to understand, to find out the American instinct. And I started reading many books on your history and culture, and on western interpretations of eastern meditation, to see how your world tries to understand mine.

Now I'm becoming more aware of the riches of the people around me. It's like discovering souls, lost dimensions in people. And the more I'm beginning to understand and reach people, the more I am giving of myself. I think it flows together, like a link. I'm feeling better and better about myself.

And I'm surprised at all the things that I have learned that I wasn't thinking about. I didn't realize that I wanted to learn American philosophy because I was lonely. I thought it was just, you know, a seeking of knowledge. But there's always a reason why you learn, isn't there? Why was I feeling sorry for myself? At first I thought I was just a silly female, not very smart but a hard worker. Now people are beginning to listen to what I say. I'm beginning to realize, I have something to offer; I am someone who can take my role and my part in this world.

I'm suddenly comfortable with people whom I was very uncomfortable with before because I thought they knew what I didn't know. Now I know we are even.

I've done a lot. I'm also suddenly aware of where I am and what my expectations are. I have a long ways to go. (Smith, 1986, p. 34)

Connie Yu had the power to break through the cultural barriers that surrounded her. She was a minority among a minority, who, with the help of a college program for working adults, was able to connect her personal experience and learning to her formal learning. That she needed to surmount barriers of prejudice and cultural ignorance should serve as a sad reminder to all Americans; that she had to do it largely on her own is a lesson to us who claim to be leaders for higher education. We have more than adequate knowledge of how to lower or eradicate most of the obstacles that Connie faced, but we are slow to act on what we know. It is easier to worry about the high rate of minority student failure.

We can't wait any longer for inclusiveness in America to move from being a value to being a fact. We are not a two- or three-race nation. More than 200 races and ethnic groups are looking to pull up chairs to our table of opportunity. And people who come from poor families and are the first in their family to attend college still face significant barriers to success. By 2020, according to the U.S. Census Bureau, 37% of the nation's population will be nonwhite. And before the freshman class of 2000 has reached retirement age, whites will constitute less than half the American workforce.

Losing Without Inclusiveness

The current loss of people, talent, and economic value signified in graduation rates below 20% is staggering. How expensive is it? We can put a price tag on the untapped economic potential that our educational system fails to develop. By some estimates, if we moved the current success rate of African-American and Hispanic students up only to that of white students, the increase in national wealth would be more than $225 billion every year (Burn, 2002). But, in human terms, it is incalculable.

Class division is also still a brutal reality for many learners in America, keeping them from the table of opportunity. Remember Bob DePrato, the self-described loser who discovered he had the capacity to learn in army training school. Here's what he had to say about actually going to college several years later.

> We had a new chief of fire prevention. Most firemen are local. His background was similar to mine. He went right up the ladder and became a Deputy Chief in a very short time. In between he dabbled in a college education and now he's right at the top. He's very successful and a nice guy. So, he convinces me that I've got to go to school . . . Like my boss told me, "You need this. It's the only way out. You're going to be wasted if you don't get this. You have to have it. I don't care how bright you are, you don't get into the club unless you wear the ring."
>
> So, I finally dragged myself over to the community college and took two courses. I was scared to death. I had been at war, in police riots, and a firefighter. That was all right. But now I'm going to this college and I literally had stomach cramps—got physically sick. I don't know why I was so scared. I could have gone there, flunked out, and nothing would have happened. I still would have been a Lieutenant in the Fire Department. As it turned out, I left there with a 4.0 after taking four courses. But when I went through the door, I was dying.
>
> I was sold this bill of goods about college, that everyone who graduated from college was far superior to the average guy walking in the street. I don't say it's a conspiracy, but I think at some level people actually peddle that attitude to keep some people out of colleges and some other people in them. Where I come from it's meant to keep them out because there's only so much room at the top. It's that simple. (Smith, 1986, p. 49)

I cannot sit through a discussion dealing with diversity, access, and quality without remembering Bob DePrato's example. This is where the friction between the student's personal, lived experience and institutional reputation and culture, the lack of fit between the tradition of higher education and the need of our society, run headlong into each other. Any program that gives a hero like Bob DePrato stomach pains because he fears failure is, itself, the failure. Anyone who believes that a college failure rate is a good measure of high quality should apply the same thinking to his local hospital and think again.

Diversity More Than a Moral Choice

Employers are stalking the gates of universities looking for graduates who mirror their customers. They want their businesses and organizations to be mirror images of the marketplaces where they deliver their products and sell their services. For them, diversity is not only a moral choice, it is also an economic imperative. In such a setting, colleges must work smarter, not just harder, to identify, recruit, enroll, and graduate an increasingly more diverse student body. Mickey Rooney wandering ivy-covered campuses in an oversized sweater may create nostalgia, but it is poor institutional modeling. We need college programs stuffed with Nagils and Mohammeds and Shareekas and Shaquilles.

We are diverse in our backgrounds, life experiences, physical abilities, ethnic traditions, age, genders, learning styles, and intelligences, among other things. In this view of the world, inclusion is not only the welcoming, ethnically balanced dormitory. It also incorporates the knowledge we have about learning, the characteristics of each learner, and the cultural assets of each learner as educational resources in the learning age. Done well, accounting for diversity and assuring inclusion strengthens the learning of both the individual student and those around her.

Love and marriage, the horse and carriage, and now quality and diversity: You can't have one without the other. Research into learning has repeatedly shown that students learn more in a multicultural environment where cultural traditions and personal experiences are explored and incorporated as part of the curriculum (Astin, 1993). Parallel research has demonstrated that engaging students in their learning, asking them to participate actively and apply the knowledge and skills they are gaining, leads to deeper and better learning. Diversity is a strength, a gift to be received with gratitude in our educational programs, our pedagogy, and our society.

If I am ever tempted to ignore this reality, I think of a class I have taught with my wife Sally in our campus's ProSeminar, where we build on the synergy unleashed by a diverse student population and new knowledge about learning. It's titled "Why We Do Things the Way We Do at CSU/MB." We spend time describing Gardner's (1983) multiple intelligence theory and engaging the students in a quick self-assessment of their own profile of multiple intelligences. This allows students to discover that each of them learns differently, and that these differences are to be expected—in fact, when we compile all the differences, and see all the different ways we learn, we have already mastered a critical lesson in inclusiveness. Sally and I want our students to understand, recognize, and appreciate the ways that they learn best as well as areas where they are not as strong, because this is the lesson that will most enable them to succeed not only at our college but throughout their lives. And we want them to see and understand the connection between how they learn and our academic structure. With this knowledge, they will be more likely to arrive at graduation day carrying with them new learning and new confidence.

Gardner's initial research describes nine intelligences that people use as they experience the world. Each has a different profile of characteristics and an accompanying style of learning. For example, people may be strong in areas of logic and verbal skill while others are more kinesthetic, visual, and interpersonal. The profiles are all equal in usefulness or value; there's no better or worse, no right or wrong profile. Each profile is given a name that describes an individual's way of experiencing the world (in other words, of learning). So, an intra-personal learner works better alone or in very small groups; he is a person who likes to figure things out for himself. Once we all know that, both the learner and those of us who are here to serve him can make the necessary adjustments. A young woman who learns in this way will now understand why group work on a large project has always been so difficult for her. The visual learner in our class suddenly blurts out memories of times when he tried and tried to learn by writing notes of lectures, but it never made sense. He failed until someone drew a picture of the truth. "If I can see it, I can get it," he says—and in his telling us this, we all get it.

If we continue to organize college as an experience primarily for people who are logical and verbal, who express themselves best through writing, who enjoy speaking in front of groups, then millions of capable students will slide out of the system wearing our label, failures. We have not yet begun applying the knowledge of the learning age. Those of us who claim the mantle of higher education leadership are far too focused on everything else: currying alumni favor, building endowments, wrestling with unions and this year's campus newspaper editor. We lose sight of what actually matters most. Those of us with the power to change higher education should hear James Carville's slightly modified advice to former President Clinton: "It's the learning, stupid!"

Branded in my mind is the image of the young Latino's hand waving in class immediately after he'd digested the meaning, for him, of Gardner's multiple intelligence theory. Eyes flashing, voice quivering, he blurted out, "Is this why I hated high school so much?" He understood, for the first time, that he had strong and weak ways of learning and that the structure of his high school had worked against his strengths. He was angry and hopeful, simultaneously full of rage and understanding. I wanted to be diplomatic, but the truthful answer to his question was: Yes. Just as there is a specific prescription for a diabetic, so there can be for different learners with different profiles. The labels he had already endured—slow and stupid—had been concocted by people who didn't know better, claiming to be wise. In fact, his struggle in high school was all about how he learned, not whether he had the intelligence and ability to learn. In high school his abilities had been ignored and denied. Our task, in college, is to capitalize on them.

Conclusion: Developing Our Assets of Inclusion and Diversity

This is where the quality of learning in the learning age lives. We must call colleges down to the street level where everyone else lives. Celebrating inclusion and diversity and engaging in active learning all begin with changes in our approach to learning. Learning-friendly colleges build all learning experiences around the learning cycle: It drives all planning for how we will incorporate personal experience and learning. Learning-friendly colleges thrive on knowing how individual students learn, knowing that we all learn differently; the profile of each student's multiple intelligences and learning style are critical to their success, and ours.

We need a sea change in colleges' assumptions about learners and communities. The change begins with understanding that learners and communities present the assets we need for powerful and deep learning, if only we're willing to integrate them into the curriculum. Remember Peg Moore. She got involved in her community because her children had chronic asthma. She was a mother, working at home, raising her children. The problem of their lives presaged a larger community problem, the lack of public health care. She founded a center, then ran a center, then returned to school where her personal learning was valued and included. Peg Moore's powerful assets came to college with her. And all of her assets would have been ignored and discounted in a traditional collegiate setting. We'd have herded her into freshman English with 100 18-year-olds.

Think of what we called urban renewal in the mid-20th century. We bulldozed ethnic communities, replacing the culture and architecture of historic but impoverished communities with new, characterless buildings. The stories and hopes and soul that had once throbbed in these communities disappeared under the bulldozer. Dignitaries arrived for ribbon cuttings, congratulating each other on what they had achieved. And what remained were buildings, not a community. We started, as we have in higher education, with the wrong set of assumptions. We called in the bulldozers because we thought of these communities as bankrupt when all they really were was poor. Blind to all their assets, we buried them, literally. Tragically, and too late, we learned that we could not get them back again.

At the Community College of Vermont we learned to build curriculum around the stated needs of learners and our shared communities. We harvested the human, physical, and programmatic resources of the community to support learning. Bankers taught about money, childcare teachers taught human development, and accountants taught math. Classes were held wherever learning was most appropriate: the bank's boardroom, the floor of the daycare center, the CPA's office. We came to think of our professional educator role as that of an educational planner who organized the communities' and individuals' resources so they could support formal learning with exceptional quality. Overall, the model was right and worked beautifully. In a comparatively poor state that had neither the population base nor the money for a string of community college campuses, we planted an appropriate technology model that built the learning program into the community, using its people, problems, buildings, and programs as the assets as the learning foundation. Quality assurance drove the design. Outcomes were everything, verifying all learning. No longer was a teacher or a classroom or a campus the definition of "college." Community-based learning was. Variations on this model, supported by the web, will work in the city centers of America as well as her rural outposts.

But it turns out that community assets are recognized not only by small community colleges in Vermont. In the 1990s, researchers at Northwestern University set out to study how the university could help its surrounding communities. They set aside $25,000 to support some worthy community group. The idea was for their chosen group to buy back any services they needed from the university in order to address community problems. A group was eventually identified; they deliberated long and hard. Finally, they returned to Northwestern with their conclusion: The university didn't have any resources that would help them solve their problems. Could they spend the money elsewhere?

I recall this story about one of America's truly splendid universities because of what happened next: The researchers agreed to the community group's request, thus beginning a learning cycle of their own. They discovered a community beyond the ivory tower that was full of people with assets, people needing respect and support. Adults in that community did not come to college with deficits to be remediated but with assets to be used. What enabled Northwestern's researchers to make these discoveries was nothing more complicated than wisdom and humility. They were willing to learn from people without college degrees and economic power. In the community's classroom, the university began its journey toward learning (Kretzmann & McKnight, 1997).

My hope is that the humility that inspired thoughtful researchers at Northwestern University to learn from the communities around the university will find its way to those of us who set higher education policies for America's future. We are on the path to failure today. We know how to succeed tomorrow. We must, in the words of Connie Yu, merely recognize that "we are even" and "we have a long ways to go" if we are going to make diversity the tie that binds America together.

7

▼

FROM WISHES TO WIRELESS:
TECHNOLOGY IN SUPPORT OF LEARNING

Diversity, in all of its manifestations, is not the only revolutionary development in our society. Technology is infusing the communities that surround our campuses, radically redefining the capacity of people and organizations, including colleges and universities, and extending the impact and the value of diversity as an asset.

Technology is transforming how we communicate and think. Our younger generations are growing up immersed in a visual experience that thoughtful observers claim is changing how they think and how they experience the world. They have grown up reading screens and searching the web through hot links, playing computer games, and learning how to think visually, logically, and analytically as they do it. These children have a different sense of themselves, their power, and their ability to interact with each other and world.

We have the capacity to throw out the traditional curriculum, to be sure. But technology also gives us the tools to let students with similar academic or curricular interests converse with and learn from each other as they do their work. And heretofore unimagined design flexibility gives both institutions and learners the capacity to break through to better teaching and learning through better alignment of learning style, intelligence, and pedagogy. We have the capacity today to redefine our use of time, space, and responsibility in a world where anyone can learn anytime and anyplace. While tradition has been maintained in schools, the world around them and the children they serve have changed dramatically. Frances Cairncross (1997) describes the breathtaking pace of change in her landmark *The Death of Distance: How the Communications Revolution Will Change Our Lives.*

> In 1943 Thomas Watson, founder of IBM, thought the world market had room for about five computers . . .

> As recently as 1967, a state-of-the-art IBM, costing $167,500, could hold a mere thirteen pages of text . . .

> The main [computer] processor on Apollo 13 contained less computing power than does a modern Nintendo games machine . . .

> A 486 chip, standard in a computer bought around 1994, could perform up to fifty-four million numerical calculations per second. A Pentium chip, the standard three years later, could perform up to two hundred million calculations per second . . . (p. 8)

The free fall in prices and dramatic expansion of computing power and reach because of the Internet, satellite communication, the use of glass fibers to carry digital signals, and chip technology have revolutionized our current relationship with technology. All this made technology cheaper and more available to the majority. Today, hundreds of millions of people can simultaneously be on telephones and computers, talking to one another around the globe. But in 1956, when the first transatlantic telephone cable went online, it had capacity for only 89 simultaneous conversations between all of Europe and all of North America (Staple, 1995).

What is most startling about all this is that Cairncross is describing what already exists, not the future. It is the environment that produced our current students, from kindergarten to medical school. This is the world of jobs into which our graduates will go, the context of business and communication and global exchange. This is the reality that hangs like a stage's backdrop, against which educators design curricula for today's learners.

Technology Supporting High-Quality Education

Technology is transforming our capacity to support high-quality learning. The opportunities for communication and deep reflection supported by technology are a source of great hope in the ability of higher education and its constituent communities—local, statewide, national or global—to effectively support significant learning. A century ago some people worried about the telephone as the device that would end all face-to-face exchanges. It was a needless worry. Similarly, the revolution in technology that has tethered us to cell phones and email has the capacity to vastly increase the interchanges between campuses and communities. I've heard the keening concerns about the disembodied world of cyberspace. But, as Cairncross (1997) suggests, "It is perverse to imagine that a technology that makes it easier to communicate should simultaneously reduce human contact" (p. 240). More to the point, it's not going away. That makes it our business to harness technology to powerful, positive uses in education.

We begin this effort, however, with a relative disadvantage. The much-discussed digital divide is sectoral as well as social and economic. And our colleges and universities are, all too often, on the far side of the divide. For example, PGA golf tournaments give scorers on the course a handheld device (a PDA) to transmit player scores, hole by hole, to an electronic master on the tournament web site. As a result, golf fans from the Philippines to Phoenix simultaneously know the status and position of every player.

Meanwhile, teachers don't know the latest information about the students in front of them, from their learning style to a head's-up from a colleague that Jimmy is having a bad day because he didn't get breakfast again. They suffocate under paperwork burdens ranging from student records to evaluations and special reports, all supported by manual filing systems just down the hall in the principal's office. Researching new curriculum ideas or accessing new teaching techniques is almost always put off to another day. Parents interested in their children's learning hope against hope that some paper will come home in the backpack. And students, who could make the computers work at the PGA golf tournaments, all too often learn in ways that Arnold Palmer did when he went to school.

Imagine what it would mean to have teachers save thousands of hours in record-keeping time, devoting those hours instead to learning activities. Technology has already made this possible.

Imagine if every learner in a school were assessed to determine how she or he learns best, and the results—a learning profile—traveled with the learner so each teacher could match pedagogy and curriculum to the learner. Quality, speed, and value of learning would skyrocket. Technology has already made this possible.

Imagine if teachers and students alike could dive deep into the Internet through multiple hotlinks to find instantaneous, vital information and to make real-life, constant applications of learning. School would suddenly become a better place to work and a better— infinitely better—place to learn. Technology has already made this possible.

Early Educational Technology: A Near Miss

I've always been an early riser. Hauling myself from bed before the sun had decently lit our Vermont home—it must have been 1972 or so—was not much of a problem. But getting up to watch TV? This was a new experience for me.

What lured me from the bedroom to the TV in our living room was something called *Sunrise Semester*. It was a breakthrough educational program produced by New York University and broadcast locally on our Burlington CBS affiliate, WCAX-TV. *Sunrise Semester*, one of the earliest and most widely recognized attempts to deliver high-quality, American liberal arts higher education to a broad audience, grew from a noble idea and a simple concept. Using television, the very best lecturers would offer their courses over the air to anyone wanting to enroll. Operating in affiliation with participating universities and colleges across the country, this would become America's classroom, an academic version of *I Love Lucy*. Curriculum material was mailed to enrollees; if they had questions, some telephone support was available through the nearest local partner, the regional college.

The noble idea behind *Sunrise Semester* was contained in the program's mission: transplanting academic excellence from a prestigious campus to the most common of living rooms. With the turn of a dial, farmers, factory workers, and housewives all had instant access to American higher education. Traveling salesmen and cops working the second shift—all were able to go to college in pajamas, or after their night shift. The regents of New York University, knowing their commitment to academic quality might be questioned, believed that the potential outweighed the risk.

In the remote regions of rural Vermont, the Community College of Vermont enrolled learners who dutifully arose at six in the morning to prepare for their class that was broadcast 30 minutes later. *Sunrise Semester* was one response to the question, "How can we deliver higher education to rural, remote populations, and do it with reasonable quality assurance?" From the student's perspective, this was a novel, unparalleled option—OK, a bit early in the morning to suit some tastes, but no earlier than the traditional milking hour for most farms.

Despite all the fanfare, learners, the main audience, were largely unimpressed. A televised talking head, even a very knowledgeable talking head, had even less pizzazz than the same talking head in person. Learning from a TV was lonely and isolated, a little boring and, well, distant. Sitting in your living room with a book and a pad, before daylight, trying to keep up with a lecture, having no way to ask a question or create a dialogue—it was possible to learn in this way, but not attractive. It was a televised version of the traditional model. One head put out and another head was supposed to take in. It was a bold try, but not a winning educational formula. *Sunrise Semester* was a near miss. But it was a miss.

Beyond higher education, however, most of American business was planning to build a future on technology by the late 1970s.

Old-style manufacturers, such as the Big Three automakers, were convinced by marketplace factors that they would need to embrace new technologies, especially in areas of communication. Subsequently, we moved from the fax to the cell phone, to the Internet, or to robotics which simultaneously reduced the need for lower-skilled labor and increased the demand for a more highly skilled workforce.

Some educators and policymakers believed it was equally imperative for education to learn how to think in terms of the new tools being developed, to embrace the potential offered by technological breakthroughs. But the embrace did not happen. The reasons varied. As a group we were, mostly, resentful and leery. Who, or what, could possibly replace the personal nature of the teaching we did?

To be fair, it takes time for successful technologies to actually get their legs with the public, let alone higher education. For example, although the telephone was invented in 1876, it was decades before it was used to communicate regularly. And although the first television transmission was in 1926, it didn't begin to take off as a widespread communication medium until the 1950s. Similarly, the first electronic computer came along in the mid-1940s, but the true revolution in technology did not truly accelerate until the 1980s.

Although the early attempts to make technology serve higher-education goals nearly always failed, even in failure they were learning projects, baby steps at the beginning of an institutional learning cycle. Educators and colleges, whether they knew it or not, were engaging the concept of harnessing the power of technology to better serve student needs. Out of failure came learning, and out of learning— and technological revolution—has come the opportunity to re-invent education and transform access to opportunity.

In business, leaders may see failure as an inevitable part of reaching for critical, competitive goals. Those businesses built on research and learning—think, for example, of the pharmaceuticals industry—know that they will see thousands of failures for one successful product. But they know that out of failure comes learning, out of learning comes knowledge, and out of knowledge comes change and success.

In education, unfortunately, failure is failure, both inside and outside the classroom. Trial and error, even if the servant of learning, is seen as a dangerous thing. Experimentation tends to be done on live subjects who are also your children. The stakes are high, and the criticism is deadly when mistakes are made public. Thus, leaders who value their careers have learned extreme caution. At almost all costs, be cautious. Be bold in promising change, but timid in making it. So, the digital divide appeared.

Technology Supporting New Learning Infrastructure

The gap between the value of technology and the needs of universities and learners represents both a lost opportunity and ground that must be regained. California State University, for example, is in the middle of a transformation of its technological infrastructure. Affecting administration, finances, and human resources operations on the administrative side, as well as creating enormous capacity for teaching and learning on the academic side, the system-wide conversion is based on two fundamental premises. First, we can't be effective, either administratively or educationally, in the 21st century without 21st-century technology to support us. Second, our students, the working and middle class students of California, many of them the first in their families to go to college, deserve a seat at the front of the education bus. So, although the capital costs have been significant, the operating costs and the increase in capacity and effectiveness, as well as opportunity for students, make it well worthwhile.

There are other examples for us to learn from. The University of Phoenix here in America and the British Open University beyond our shores both serve tens of thousands of students who simultaneously work and lead regular lives while engaged in degree programs. Both programs represent important examples of quality-assured postsecondary education that relies on technology and other nontraditional support strategies to provide high-quality learning services that are responsive to learners' needs in thousands of settings. After years of research and trial and error, these institutions, and others like them, are serving new clienteles effectively and responsively.

Are these examples anomalies or the leading edge of a new wave of institutional types and formats? The venerable *Chronicle of Higher*

Education broke the story in a single sentence in 2001: "In the past 13 years, while more than 100 four-year colleges in the United States have closed, the number of corporate universities has ballooned from 400 to more than 2,000" (Meister, 2001, p. B10). We who are paid to lead higher education have known a trend was underway. We have probably underestimated its depth, its power, and its size. We have failed to reckon with the reality that, in the learning age, we have no monopoly over the business of higher education. We no longer control the reward structure, the meaning of degrees and certificates, or the definitions of quality. We are sometimes the institutional pipelines to America's workforce, but increasingly we are not. We are sometimes the holders of critical and competitive knowledge, but increasingly we are not.

At California State University–Monterey Bay, we operate in a wireless environment, requiring technological literacy in our general education program. With our outcomes-based curriculum, our learners have to demonstrate that they not only can use, but also understand how and why the information technology works before proceeding to upper-division work in their major area of study. As part of our university learning requirements, the outcomes for our general education program, every lower-division student has to demonstrate technological literacy before advancing to the upper-division program. The key component to this requirement is either an assessment course which allows students to successfully demonstrate their capacity without taking the course or our core course, Tech Tools, which is available either online or in a class-based/laboratory format. Why did we make technological literacy a requirement? Because we believe that, in our students' lives, not having that capability will be equivalent to not knowing how to read and write.

Whether technology is seen as a way of protecting tradition or changing it, technology itself can no longer be resisted by those who teach or those who fund teaching, because it is now as basic to learning as the ABCs. The chasm must be crossed, and can be crossed, if we have leaders willing to take the necessary risks. Now is the time to close the gap between the haves and have-nots; now is the time to cross the chasm between our campuses and the rest of the society. It will take an investment not only of money, but also of courage, inventiveness, and knowledge about learning. It will demand that a consensus emerge between policymakers, lawmakers, taxpayers, educators, and leaders in business and the media. And it will require leadership.Respected voices need to be heard on this issue, championing the change.

Technology Supporting Partnering

In the learning age successful colleges will be those that are effective at partnering with other community-based institutions, including employers. The workplace will be seen as an important laboratory for learning with actual, paid-for work at the core of the curriculum. In this conception, the community itself is a learning center filled with authentic learning assets from which we take lessons in every imaginable field including sociology, economics, communication, and criminal justice. Colleges will increasingly draw on the knowledge and experience of their learners as assets. And the World Wide Web will serve as a tool available to support learning 24/7/365, enabling us to go from high-tech to high-teach to lifelong learning.

A vivid illustration of colleges embracing both common sense and community need was recently offered when California State University decided to do something about a terrible problem in California's schools. Over 15% of California's teachers are provisionally certified. In plain terms that means they are teaching without a certificate. More bluntly, that means they are not qualified for this most important of all professions. Still, there they are in the schools, usually with our highest-need students, teaching every day. Part of our mission is to assist in the improvement of K–12 education. With analysis we decided several things:

- The problem was not going away. Despite all we were doing to train new teachers, we would not be able to staff California's classrooms with a fully qualified teacher for every child using traditional methods.

- These marginally prepared teachers were not coming to our programs for further professional training and development as the law required.
- They were becoming a permanent fixture in California's classrooms.
- Each of these teachers, though not fully trained, had made a commitment to children and the profession, had voted with their feet and their time. They were in the classrooms already.
- We knew who they were and where they were.

We analyzed this situation as a 21st-century work and learning problem. Unlike some corporate employers, we could not solve the problem with visas, lobbyists, or imported resources. There was neither time nor money to remove people from the workplace and send them back to school in the traditional ways.

These teachers could not afford to leave work for school, but we couldn't have them continue work without school. So, we created a technologically supported teaching credential program which uses their workplace and work experience everyday as the core of the curriculum. Using the appropriate technology of their daily work, we created a customized training program, CalState TEACH (http://www.calstateteach.net/public/home.html) that moved away from the traditional one-size-fits-all model for teacher preparation.

Each teacher's daily work organizer, the lesson plan, became the reference point for the curriculum. Enrolled teacher-students were asked to link their ongoing lesson planning and teaching to the state standards their students needed to meet and also to the best known teaching practices. With technological support, we created access to the necessary information and also put the students in touch with each other to discuss problems and issues through chat rooms. At the same time, they have electronic access to an expert mentor and they receive regular observation in their classrooms. Learning is individualized and connecting directly to the work teacher-students do everyday.

CalState TEACH is built on the needs of individual learners matched to resources that were present in the community. The program itself emerged because learners and employers, policymakers, and business and political leaders demanded that their colleges become learner-friendly, use existing technologies, and focus less on traditional teaching methodology and more on effective learning strategies. Learning standards were certainly not lowered; probably, they were raised. And it was all accomplished by leaving behind the one-size-fits-all pedagogical concept. No one was herded into a lecture hall to have knowledge dispensed to him or her. On the contrary, what our teacher-students already knew and were doing was the basis for continued learning. CalState TEACH is a workplace-based, web-supported, professional education that converts time and work into learning. It has higher quality ratings than the average ratings of campus-based traditional programs. The major complaint? It's too rigorous (California State University, 2002)!

Why does CalState TEACH succeed where *Sunrise Semester* failed? For one thing, we have exponentially greater technological capacity today. We no longer think of cell phones and PCs as the hardware of a few; they are as ordinary as SUVs and CD players. We have grown comfortable with, and dependent upon, flexible, powerful technology.

Sunrise Semester had to ask that people set aside their home or career or other activities to learn; CalState TEACH is able to integrate the learning into the learner's life. They continue to work and, thanks to technology, get a second value out of their work: learning.

Technology is a great learning tool when it is interactive, and those of us staring at *Sunrise Semester* early in the morning were not so much learners as listeners and viewers. We were just supposed to take it in. What we now know about learning is that just taking it in doesn't work very well for many, many people. First, you lose students who drop the course. And second, those who complete it don't retain much of what they learned.

What technology now enables us to do—what CalState TEACH can do that *Sunrise Semester* could not—is engage the learner, personalize attention, improve communication, and increase instant exposure to world-class information and learning when the learner wants it. This technology is not a substitute for teaching; it's an extension, a means to a better, more efficient, more effective purpose: learning.

Technology Supporting Learning

Splendid teaching can occur in the most traditional of classrooms. But even splendid teaching in a traditional setting is isolated from the support and added value that technology adds. For a moment, think of teaching and learning as a bundle of things that we've traditionally done. We've prepared curriculum and delivered it. We've kept attendance, reviewed student work, assessed it, graded it, reported on it. We've talked with learners, more often than not in groups (we ordinarily see learners in classes); we've asked how they are doing. We've performed research, developed new knowledge, integrated it into our teaching. We've tried to adjust our methods to match our students within these constraints.

Technology turns the model inside out, promoting a great increase in splendid learning. Successful technologically supported models take the elements of teaching and learning and re-bundle them, organizing them differently. A curriculum is still provided, but it is not housed solely in books and a syllabus. Information is still delivered to the learner, but it does not all come from one person or one voice, in one place, and at the same time every week. Instead of having every class begin with what we will be teaching today, learning is frequently initiated by the learner who is seeking knowledge about what's happening around him, now; and the information she seeks is immediately applied to her situation. Evaluations are still done (but more thoroughly, because computing power is greater than grading power). Reporting is still done (but more completely, because computing makes possible faster, deeper, more individualized accountability). The work of guided, higher-level learning is being done because the key elements of learning have been re-bundled in ways that capitalize on greater knowledge of how people learn and greater use of computing power.

A good example of a developing primary resource for teachers and learners who want to re-bundle the curriculum and gain the support of technology is MERLOT, the Multimedia Educational Resource for Online Teaching. Created initially by educators who wanted to collaborate, evaluate, and disseminate online curricula, MERLOT is a dynamic repository of curricula, complete with evaluations and comments by those who have used it, available to any faculty member or learner who wants to become a member. MERLOT has evolved into an internationally accepted online resource. Here's how it works.

> Almost all the information contained in MERLOT has been added by the people who use MERLOT. The users of MERLOT write the descriptions of the learning materials, learning assignments, user comments, peer reviews, and member profiles following web-based forms. To contribute materials to the MERLOT collection, user must become a MERLOT Member, which is free and easy to do. MERLOT has also created discipline-based editorial boards whose responsibility includes expanding, organizing, reviewing, and generally managing the collection of learning materials and support resources. Each year, the MERLOT project plans to add editorial boards in new discipline areas.

> MERLOT conducts peer review of online learning materials, a process that will help insure that learning materials within the MERLOT collection address significant theoretical or research issues are contextually accurate, pedagogically sound, and technically easy to use. MERLOT has modeled its peer reviews on the discipline-based peer review of scholarship and research. MERLOT's peer review process also provides a mechanism for professional recognition for faculty developing and using instructional technology. MERLOT has a second and parallel review process that complements the formal peer reviews. Individual MERLOT members can provide their observations and evaluations on the learning materials within MERLOT.

> MERLOT has also created Discipline Community websites which are subsets of the whole MERLOT collection that are focused on specific disciplines. Search-

ing and browsing within these communities returns
results only within that discipline. These communities
also represent the subject areas in which MERLOT
Editorial Boards conduct peer review of materials.
MERLOT has recently created Discipline Community
websites such as MERLOT-CATS (Community for
Academic Technology Staff) and MERLOT-Teaching
and Technology. MERLOT-CATS focuses on sharing
tools, methods and expertise among academic computing support staff. Authors of online materials will find
useful tools and techniques here as well. MERLOT-
Teaching and Technology is designed to aid faculty and
faculty development professionals in their planning
for successfully using online resources in teaching and
learning. (http://taste.merlot.org)

Technology hands us new tools every day that will allow us to
reach new populations and employ new knowledge about learning
with new effectiveness and unimagined quality. But tapping into this
new capacity will require a rethinking of the enterprise of education
including the economics and the structure of universities.

To quote again from Cairncross (1997), the day is approaching
when the parents and payers of America's college students will

> grow restive at the cost of university education. In 1995
> private universities in the United States effectively
> charged each student nearly $60 per lecture—a figure
> that will have since increased and that did not take ac-
> count of either public or private support. Yet one sur-
> vey of consumers found that only about 31 percent felt
> that college tuition gave "good" or even "average" value
> for the money. Technologically supported learning may
> not yet have the cachet of a good university name, but
> it is already as good as, and less expensive than, a me-
> diocre one. (p. 274)

Although we would all prefer to be better than mediocre, Cairncross has described the minimum standard for technologically supported learning: better than mediocre. Our predicament reminds me of the story about the two men who came across a mountain lion one day while hiking. Terrified, they ran as fast as they could. As the lion gained on them, one fellow said to his pal, "What are we doing? We can't outrun that mountain lion?" To which his friend replied, "I don't have to outrun the mountain lion, I only have to outrun you!"

In truth, I believe that Cairncross is conservative in her assessment of the costs that the society will be increasingly unwilling to bear. I believe we will be increasingly unwilling to bear the social cost of failing to successfully educate those we are currently leaving behind. Furthermore, the costs associated with having higher education removed from the workplace and the community, let alone the living room, will also become unacceptable to many.

Conclusion: Technology and Synergy

Our rapidly expanding technological capacity allows us, today, to do an infinitely more individualized, more effective job at educating. It gives educators far greater control with significantly increased flexibility to interpret traditional uses of time, space, and responsibility to deliver learning services more effectively.

As the extraordinary capacity of technology is combined with the convergence of demographic forces and new knowledge about learning, it creates uncommon synergy. Even as we discuss and analyze their impact, these forces are transforming America's educational landscape by creating a new learning ethos. Our continuing error, however, has been to consider them separately, ignoring their synergy. Such thinking undoes us. These are not autonomous issues, separable from one another. You cannot separate a learner's cultural background, his intelligence profile, and her aspirations from the value of technology or how he learns because those elements don't operate separately in people's lives. Each is a strand that, taken together, makes up a thread woven through our society. And they are redefining the ethos of learning and higher education in America.

"Synergy" is a biological term defined as the action of two or more substances, organs, or organisms, to achieve an effect of which each is individually incapable. By itself, technology cannot save us. Taken separately, new populations of students might continue to stymie us. And, considered in a vacuum, new learning models for organizations and individuals might not dramatically improve higher education's impact. But if we understand and anticipate the synergy of the social, technological, economic, and political forces at work around us, employing them together, it will be possible to achieve what none of these forces can deliver alone.

Historically, higher education has controlled its world by controlling its workforce, its curriculum content, and its certification/ reward structure. But this de facto structural monopoly of authority and responsibility is being broken as new types of institutions hire new types of faculty, offer new academic models and degree programs in the workplace and on personal time, and harness technology to supplement and support learning anytime, anyplace. Why are programs like MERLOT, CalState TEACH, and the University of Phoenix doing what they are doing? The answer is as simple as it is profound. Because the service is needed and because they can.

As we look ahead to the year 2025, higher education must get over the conceit that traditional institutions, organizational structures, and services will control the future development of higher educational services as they have in the past. The synergy generated by the emerging forces is not controlled by institutions, it is embedded in the surrounding communities, outside their walls. In 20 years, the education mainstream is going to look very different from the way it looks today. Programs, practices, and services that operate on the margins of higher education today, or have not been invented, will migrate to its center. And services and combinations of resources not yet conceived will dot the center of the education landscape.

PART THREE
FUTURETHINK

8

▼

FutureThink: A New Mainstream

The very term "mainstream" suggests a location on the spectrum, a middle ground where accepted activities occur and where, by implication, the risk is less. In 20 years, there will still be millions of students learning on college campuses all over America. There will still be faculty. There will still be organized curricula. But how the students are doing their learning, where they do it, and how that learning is supported will be dramatically different, as will be the expectations that we, and they, have for their learning. The new mainstream will also, however, redefine the current scope of responsibility and authority in higher education, including other locations like the workplace, the home, the learning cooperative, and the community as equal partners in the learning society of the future.

"Mainstream" also suggests a set of accepted practices and services—assured, confidence-inspiring institutional forms, programs, and support services that comprise and characterize this safe place. In the new mainstream, campuses will no longer have the sole authority and responsibility for teaching and learning. Learning, its validation, and its support will be shared far beyond today's conception of the campus. By 2025, we will have invented, tested, and validated the organizational and educational effectiveness of myriad new practices and services that populate the mainstream. And quality assurance will have moved beyond the accreditation practices of the 1990s, found to be so out-of-sync with the emerging field of practice.

In this closing section, I will take a look into the future, discussing new locations, practices, organizational forms, and quality assurance issues using vignettes about how learning might occur in 2025. Focusing on one place, the workplace (Chapter 8), and on one service, quality assurance (Chapter 9), I will use the vignettes to introduce the possible combinations of services and pedagogies that will populate the mainstream in 2025. Then, in Chapter 10, I will discuss the assumptions that should lie behind policy considerations for the future.

From Workplace to Learnplace

Something is wrong in America's workplaces. The world's most productive economy can't seem to find its balance when it comes to preparing and maintaining a capable workforce. Educators and policymakers are beset by stories of graduates entering the workforce who can't cut the mustard. And parents fret that their children, even with a college degree, won't be able to hold and progress in a job after graduating from college.

The discussion of the disconnect between higher education and the workplace usually goes something like this.

- **For higher education:** Alas, the ideal of a liberally educated person is under relentless and insurmountable pressure. With the demographic expansion of the student base and the drive for increased access, it's impossible to protect the standards and the practices of the liberal ideal. And, we can't afford it anyway. The economics just aren't there. We have vocationalized our curriculum to the point where it cannot possibly serve the desirable objectives of liberal education. Train or educate, that's our dilemma. Students and their parents want job preparation, not a liberal education. And the marketplace is echoing their refrain. We are trapped in a Hobson's choice: Be true to our past or serve the marketplace of incoming students and employer demands.

- **For business:** I don't know where you think you are succeeding. But wherever it may be, it surely isn't the marketplace. Your graduates can't read or write, and they can't apply concepts in the workplace. They don't understand the global marketplace or the diversity of evolving customer bases. They can't analyze problems and think critically. They don't know how to think ethically and work on teams. We have to retrain them for the reality of work. I don't know what you think you are doing, but preparing your graduates for the workplace isn't part of it.

These are not new arguments. Nor are they particularly helpful. We need to succeed at both intellectual development and workforce preparation. The workplace of the future needs broadly educated people who know culture as well as calculus, who know how to learn again and again and again. The most sought-after employee is the one who can be at home in Toledo or Toronto or Tokyo, affirming—not clashing with—the local culture, advancing the mission of her or his employer in the new marketplace.

A high-quality education in the 21st century can deliver employability as well as intellectual development. We can write learning outcomes for a course on Hemingway that include learning how to write better and think more critically while also learning the great author's masterpieces, combining conscious learning of content with learning of deeper intellectual capacity. We don't need to first study reading, then writing, then Hemingway. Similarly, we can write learning outcomes for a chemistry course that include analytic thinking and research methodology on issues of public health as well as the principles of chemistry. And then we can infuse both learning experiences with structured experiential learning experiences, internships, service-learning assignments, and jobs that ground the learners' work in the reality of the workplace experience.

So, what might a curriculum that gave learners the intellectual

development for a life of continuing learning while also preparing them
for the workplace actually look, and feel, like in the years ahead?

*Sam Hudnut was not happy, not happy at all! As the leader of the Gray Team,
he had been working for three months on the marketing problem faced by the
National Author's Center (NAC) in nearby Roseville. The NAC, a leading
regional nonprofit, was in trouble. Despite its deep array of resources and exhibits, featuring all of the authors from the region, NAC couldn't get customers
through the front door to experience its exhibits. And sales in the NAC store
were stagnant. All this when tourism was up and the surrounding communities were growing. Sam, a junior in Sequoia State University's (SSU) School of
Business, was leading a team of four students that was charged with preparing
marketing recommendations to stop the slide for the center's administration
and board.*

*And now, just two weeks before the board meeting, Louisa Harcourt, the
NAC's executive director, had dismantled his team's report, piece by piece. She
didn't like what the team had produced, saying that it wasn't what she had
asked for, that it only described the shape and size of the hole NAC was in, but
didn't get them a ladder to climb out of it. As the meeting ended, Harcourt had
reminded Sam of her first rule of holes. "Sam," she had said. "Remember: When
you are in a hole, the first rule is to stop digging!" The Gray Team had 14 days
to get it right. They were on the board agenda at the spring 2025 meeting.*

*As Louisa's image faded from his interactive computer, and still reeling
from her critique, Sam tried to piece the situation together. He wished some of
the other team members had been at the meeting to hear the critique, but he
hadn't thought there would be a need. The draft report was a superb analysis of
the problem the NAC faced. With graphs and charts backed up by analysis and
research in marketing, they had described specifically and clearly the NAC's
situation, including customer analyses about what worked and what didn't
at the center, from several focus groups. They had brought the best literature
in marketing to bear on the problem, with excellent references and clear argu-
mentation.*

*As he churned and reflected, Sam thought, "Well, maybe we did
lean a little too heavily on Allie. But she was so eager to do her analysis. And her ability to prepare the presentation was so good." It had seemed
like a reasonable thing to do. Now, the four of them were going to have to
start all over again in order to succeed in solving the NAC's problem.*

As he approached the school's cafeteria, Louisa's parting shot still rang in Sam's ears: "Stop digging!"

The team would have to start at the beginning and rethink the project and the problem. This six-month learning project, Developing Marketing Solutions, addressed several of the learning outcomes required for graduation in business, including knowing and applying principles of marketing, customer satisfaction, and teamwork in a specific situation. Their presentation to the board and the board's reaction was a huge part of the course evaluation because they were the clients! Sam was involved with three other projects, but luckily none of them were scheduled for completion in the next three weeks. Silently he issued up thanks for the living/learning community at SSU, a community where most of the students worked and lived and also went to school. The curriculum was year-round and the learning experiences were staggered to adapt to the differing schedules of the students. Nonetheless, the Gray Team had its work cut out for it.

Three weeks later, as he looked back on it, Sam realized that the breakthrough had initially come from Maria, the quietest member of the team. In the meeting that followed Louisa Harcourt's critique, Maria had suggested that, in their excitement with understanding and presenting the analysis of the problem, the team had actually gotten sidetracked from its original goal. She continued that for every characteristic of the problem they had identified, there should be a recommendation about how to actually change the marketing program as well as the in-house offerings at NAC to connect not only with the surrounding communities, but also with the tourists who visited, generating increased traffic and sales. And the team was launched on a frenzy of work to reframe their report to the board.

Using their web chat room and links to marketing best practices and case study web sites, the team searched for approaches that fit the situation they were working. At the same time, they met, individually and collectively with several business mentors in the community as well as their overall project leader, George Ledyard, a marketing executive from the area who was teaching part-time at SSU. And they frequented the business education center on the SSU campus repeatedly, in search of advice from other faculty and students alike.

It had been an intense two weeks, fitting all this extra work into already-busy schedules of work and learning projects. Long days. Weekends. But it had been worth it. Three days before the board meeting, the team had presented the conceptual outline of its findings to Louisa. Building on the analysis they *had done, the team members were, among other things, recommending major changes in the NAC's web site and web marketing, a renewed focus on families and children, including family days at the NAC, and developing a series of three-dimensional electronic children's games that would encourage reading and writing about elements of a child's daily life based on the literature in the center.*

Their proposed overall strategy was to move the visitor from observer to participant/partner, engaging them in the value of the center. The team's ability to hotlink each recommendation to examples of best practice at other nonprofits, while also connecting its analysis to the marketing rationale and anticipated pro formas, made the presentation complete. Louisa had been relieved and very pleased. And the board had adopted several of their recommendations, tasking Louisa and the rest of the center administration with developing the programs.

In one light moment, a board member had asked where they were going to get the expertise to develop their web site and the games. And Sam had replied that there were several students in the media and technology program at Sequoia State who might be able to help.

Later, as they debriefed with Ledyard, the team members reflected on the real problem they had confronted and the real learning they had done. They had known the marketing concepts, how to employ the incredible resources of I3, the new multidimensional Internet with mode- and task-integrating capacity, and how to access the advice and support from professors, mentors, and other students. They had figured out how to research game theory and recommend ideas for games. But they had spent a lot of their early work effort focusing on the wrong aspect of the problem—the analysis and presentation—instead of the solution. In the end, their proposals—in content, form, and alignment—had addressed the expressed needs of the NAC. And each of them had another example in his or her portfolio to show prospective employers when they entered the job market.

What They Learned

Sam and the Gray Team confronted their accountability to their customer. They learned how to think, and through the project, they transcended the principles of marketing that they had learned from a book by applying those principles, along with their natural intelligence, in a real-world situation. Their work exemplifies many of the characteristics that employers say they need in college graduates. Their work also exemplifies several of the intellectual characteristics of a well-educated, liberal arts graduate. These include:

- The ability to think critically and analytically
- The ability to solve problems by applying information and knowledge across different situations
- The ability to work effectively on teams, to collaborate and achieve consensus
- The ability to reach comfortably across cultural and ethnic traditions
- The ability to understand domestic and global co-workers and customers, write effectively, and read broadly
- The ability to employ technology as a second language

How to Promote New Learning

To prepare and offer a curriculum such as this one, universities need to take the following steps:

- Develop specific learning outcomes for the general education program and each major and minor.
- Organize learning resources to develop the capacity in each learner to achieve and demonstrate those learning outcomes.
- Develop a network of learning sites in the community where students are welcome to participate.
- Develop an IT infrastructure that allows for all curricular material to be available on the net, including hotlinks and URLs for other source areas.
- Equip students with appropriate computing power to use their time and talent effectively.
- Organize, train, and assign mentors to every learning team.
- Use professors' time for problem solving and consultation, not simply presentation.

These elements require a rethinking of university organizational structures and resource allocation patterns. They move sharply away from the one-size-fits-all class and lecture format, evaluated by papers and tests, where the vast preponderance of the university experience is prearranged. And they prepare the university to migrate organizationally from the mass production mode toward a design-build mode that is more responsive to the needs of the learners.

In this conception, the resources of the university are variables, available for the design and support of the curriculum and student learning. The learning outcomes, the results, are the constants. With this approach the university develops more flexibility to design learning programs for students that combine content, the development of workplace-friendly perspectives, and experiences that, upon reflection, create meaning as well as knowledge. Most importantly, quality is based on the outcomes, not the inputs. Budding computer scientists can wire schools and create web pages for nonprofits. Biology majors can analyze community health problems for neighborhood groups while teachers-in-waiting read to elementary school students. Students can master the content of a degree program while explicitly developing and demonstrating the intellectual and behavioral traits of a liberally educated person.

Our students won't have to choose between preparation for work and a liberal education, because college can educate you with both.

Needed: A Partnership

Higher education and business are standing on tiptoes looking over the walls of tradition toward a historic opportunity for a partnership. If they are interested and willing, universities and the business community can form alliances that make available lifelong, workplace-based, community-based learning in the workplace of the future. That workplace will be characterized by increased knowledge, increasingly sophisticated information and equipment, and higher workforce mobility.

New Knowledge

Increasingly complex knowledge requirements characterize increasingly sophisticated organizations. In 1998, no less than 69% of the nation's companies suggested that a lack of skills was a barrier to their potential growth. Thirty-nine percent of the current workforce and 26% of new hires have basic skill deficiencies. And even during the 2002 economic downturn, nearly half of all employers (46%) reported difficulty in finding qualified workers (Heldrich, 2002).

NEW INFORMATION AND EQUIPMENT

Capital investment in educational facilities is a growing problem. The hard reality is that American business and industry vastly out-invest colleges in capital development. The rate of innovation and development in our private sector has made a shambles of the investment cycle traditionally used by colleges for ideas, facilities, laboratories, and technology. Many of our students are learning old formulations on outdated machines and technology. By the time we get a new curriculum or facility planned, bought, paid for, and open, it is out of date. This has the logic of designing a parking structure with horse stalls in it. We need an educational model that increasingly uses the workplace as the learnplace to close this gap.

INCREASED MOBILITY

Finally, the mobility of the American workforce has increased dramatically. The more highly skilled we are, the more likely we are to move from place to place and job to job. About one-fourth of all American workers have been with their current employer for 12 months or less (U.S. Bureau of Labor Statistics, 2002). And our graduates will hold more than seven jobs in multiple industries over their careers. This evolving and dynamic version of work is a far cry from that which shaped American society during the first 200 years of our history.

Over the last 75 years, the American workplace has evolved from a predictable and stable sector to one whose major characteristic is dynamic change with productivity measured against global standards. In this kind of economy, American colleges and universities must educate people to achieve ongoing, high-performance learning. It will be personal learning, adapted to the style of learning that works best for each individual. It will be continuous learning because the world in which we live is continuously changing. The new minimum workforce requirement is for graduates with real-world experience who can continue to learn.

Listen to Joe Lamell as he illustrates linking the intellectual with the practical by looking back on his three tours of duty in Vietnam where he inherited recurring waves of college-educated second lieutenants.

> I've trained these people, I did three tours in 'Nam. I didn't think I was God, but I knew what I was doing, and I didn't feel that, with eight or nine years in, that somebody coming out of boot camp with a bar on was going to tell me what I was supposed to be doing.
>
> A lot of the difference was that they were book-learned, book-taught. They had it upstairs and they figured they could go out and assault a hill using the book. And, you know, you just didn't do all things that way. I mean, it's great to be able to teach certain things by the book, but when it comes to actual combat and preparing a person for a combat situation, you have got to teach them the know-how, the basic idea of staying alive. It comes in awful handy . . .
>
> An awful lot of men over there in Vietnam never saw the end of the first month because they were so smart.
>
> They were "book-taught" but not battle ready. (Smith, 1986, p. 27)

We have long since stopped sending our youth to Vietnam but we continue to send them into communities and the workplace as unequipped as Joe Lamell's "second lights" for the reality that faces them.

To fill this gap, business is investing heavily in training. Already some 45 million adults annually participate in some type of work-related training. And, in 1999 alone, American businesses invested at least $62 billion in new and continuing employee training. They made the investment because they had no choice. If they want to be competitive, they need competent employees.

And business is also looking for skilled workers in foreign markets. It is faster, cheaper, easier, and less frustrating to demand that members of Congress open the borders, increasing the quota of H1B visas to satisfy the demand for equipped workers. In 2002 alone, the U.S. government authorized up to 195,000 H1B visas to meet the skills shortage faced by some American employers. Importing the skilled workforce to compensate for our educational failures is, however, a double-edged sword. It is a safety valve for businesses, allowing them to compensate for the failures of American education. But it also subsidizes the failure of education ignoring the victims of that failure and masking the long-term consequences for our society.

A higher education–business alliance that combined the value of current and projected business investments in training with the value of current and projected higher education investment in postsecondary education would transform both parties as well as the learning opportunities for millions of Americans. How might such an alliance work, look, and feel? Consider the case of Lionel James and his daughter, Esther.

Lionel James was worried. As he paced in his den, concern flickered through his mind. He was proud of his degree from Larkin State University. The first in his family to get a degree, he had walked across the stage in 1974 after five and one-half years, found a company with a great entry-level training program, and was off to the races.

But now, 30 years later, his oldest daughter, Esther, was following a very different path. And he was worried. After high school and a year at the local community college, she had joined VISTA for a year, ending up in St. Louis at the YWCA where she worked as a staff assistant to the director for four years. Now she had come home to work and get her degree.

Farragut County, the economic hub of eastern Iowa's economic renaissance, had developed a workplace-based degree network called the common market in which six colleges and universities as well as members of the Chamber of Commerce and the Business Council worked together to turn all of Farragut County's workplaces into learning laboratories. In the common market, all learning, regardless of the sponsor or the provider, was assessed and credit applied toward agreed-upon learning outcomes for the different degree programs that were offered. To achieve this, university and human resource departments worked together to develop and align their offerings with degree and certificate outcomes and requirements so that students could apply the value of both to their work and their learning. It was a learning/working ladder that anyone could climb.

It confused Lionel, because Farragut County's common market had nothing to do with a specific campus, or five and a half years. Even though Larkin State was a member, Lionel was worried. He remembered going to class at eight in the morning, studying at the library, grinding for finals, watching athletic events, and working on the side, delivering newspapers every morning.

But Esther wasn't doing any of that. She told him that work was her campus, and she talked casually about linked discussions, learning objectives, and assessed learning. Would it be good enough for her? Was it worth anything? What was it?

Hearing her footfalls on the front steps, Lionel steeled himself for the conversation to come . . . and, as she settled herself on the couch, Esther began to answer his questions with a torrent of excited words.

"Oh, Daddy, it is different, but it's so cool! The FCCM (Farragut County Common Market) has enrolled me in a semester-long assessment class to give me advanced standing for all of the learning I did as a VISTA and at the "Y" in St. Louis. It's a new form of advanced placement. Using their learning outcomes and assessment rubrics, I have a chance to get some credit for what I already know! And I'll get credit for the year I spent at Admiral Community College before I went into VISTA. And my student identification card also acts as a one-stop card. It gets me access to any library, facility, or sanctioned event that is sponsored by any of the partners. The FCCM has many more resources together than any one of the institutions does alone. There are speakers and events all the time and they're all open to me."

She rushed on, "All my learning work is done at the office. The FCCM has degree programs that include all approved business-based courses as well as courses from all of the participating colleges and organizations. All approved courses count toward the degree and it all comes together at work!"

Esther's words tumbled out. "Some of my courses are actually organized around the work we are doing. My supervisor has given me a work plan for the year, emphasizing areas where she wants me to strengthen my performance and specific tasks she wants me to fulfill. The FCCM lets me make that work plan part of my learning plan for the year.

"A lot of my 'homework' involves doing my job and then studying, thinking, and talking with others to figure out how to do it better. No, I don't have any lecture courses, but with the online immediate access wireless link, I can access any content, chat room, or work through the curriculum to web-based resources that help me with the problems I'm trying to solve. And we organize discussion groups around lunchtimes and on the weekends. The best part is the chat room of other learners who are studying the same material. We share problems and perceptions, as well as solutions with each other all the time. If I need

help from an expert, it's only a click and an appointment away!"

Overwhelmed, if not entirely convinced, Lionel shook his head. His daughter, all of 26 years old, was describing a new world. Impressed with her enthusiasm and focus, he shrugged his shoulders in resignation and, with an inward smile, reminded himself that he hadn't ever been able to say no to her anyway.

Programs like the Farragut County Common Market are possible today. The Esther James of America shouldn't have to wait until 2025. If collegiate planners redefined our higher education role around co-operation, co-investment, and applied learning that equips graduates for service and work, we would reshape our student bodies, revitalize our learning programs, and renew the American marketplace. In a world where "working smarter" is the watchword, employers and learners no longer need a partner whose focus is preemployment; they need a partner in lifelong learning that covers lifetimes.

There is no more profound example of this changing dynamic than the information technology field. Clifford Adelman, a senior research analyst with the U.S. Department of Education, studied the business-education ties in the information technology field. His conclusion confirms what we know but have, in higher education circles, steadfastly refused to accept:

> *. . . at the center of this postsecondary system of teaching, learning, and credentialing is not the local institution but the global student.* We can call it "postsecondary" because the level of reading, reasoning, and communication skills necessary to comprehend and apply its content assumes secondary-level education in most countries. It is the student who, on entering that system, negotiates different sources and ways of learning without being bound to any institution in any given place in any given country. And, what distinguishes this system most from the academic world is that it operates the same way, with the same signals to students, and with the same meanings, in Montreal, Manaus,

Munich, Mogadishu, Manila, Moscow, and Milwaukee. (Adelman, 2000, p. 29)

This suggests the need for a new array of institutional services
and practices similar to those used by Sam and Esther. Consider this.
Adelman's global student doesn't fit our current conception of who
a college student is. Moving around, in and out of college courses,
and in and out of work situations, the student is gaining experience,
knowledge, and skills from life, from courses, from work, and from
in-service offerings. But she has no one place to collect that learning,
have it assessed and valued, and put it to work. She has no way to
create the coherence to her learning or the experience of engaging in
learning that, historically, the college campus experience provided and
then reported on its transcript. She needs an assessment-based mobile
transcript, a learning passport that travels with her, reflects the learning
she has done, and validates her skills and knowledge for employers and
colleges alike. Like the turtle with its house on its back, each worker
would carry validation of their experience, skills, and ability. And
employers would be able to depend on the claims of skill, competence,
and knowledge that the mobile transcript carried.

A Partnership That Struggled
We can link learning and working far more closely. Here's one example
of a good workforce education and training program that has been
significantly underutilized because of mobility, distance, and a lack of
partnership. The Congress, seeing a link between the military's assets and
the nation's educational needs, developed a program called Troops to
Teachers in the early 1990s. It was a simple concept. Soldiers preparing
to leave the service would be equipped to convert their experience,
training, and discipline into teaching careers. This would be a wonderful
new source of teachers, bringing highly qualified, experienced teachers
who would also be good role models into thousands of American
classrooms. The concept was simple: Troops leaving the armed services
would be given priority treatment to gear them toward teaching and
then employ them in school districts where more and better teachers
were needed.

Unfortunately, the dominant model of our teacher training

programs and the hiring practices and calendars of school districts have combined to frustrate the program's success. Teachers need to be trained before they can go into a classroom. Training costs money. So, interested candidates discovered that they had to attend school for months, up to a year, after discharge from the military before being able to get into a classroom. As a result, the economics of going to school without having a paycheck seriously wounded the program's success. And no one yet has thought to bring the teacher preparatory courses to the soldiers and sailors via the web prior to their discharge or to educate them on the job afterward. So, although the idea is splendid, it has failed to thrive with large numbers. Ironically, experience with the program, though limited, confirms that returning troops are indeed a great source of qualified teachers and that they can make the leap to classroom teaching (National Center for Education Information, 1998). But the traditions of higher education and the failure to work cooperatively with school districts and the military have been a serious obstacle to the program's success.

And One That Didn't

The CalState TEACH web-based teacher training curriculum anticipated this particular transition problem of linking personal economics, workforce need, and training. The program targeted teachers who were already employed on emergency certificates and needed a permanent credential. They were receiving a paycheck, already had the classroom as a learning laboratory, and had the incentive to become fully certified. We then wrapped the training around the workplace, using the classroom as a learning laboratory. Learning and working were integrated.

Participants have consistently rated CalState TEACH higher than the averages for other CSU teacher training programs. Interestingly, when they were asked what part of the curriculum was most helpful in supporting their learning, the teachers chose peer education: what they had learned from each other in chat rooms that were especially designed for the curriculum. In other words, the chance to build community and to share experiences and perspectives with each other, based on the common experience of teaching and participating in the curriculum, were leading educational resources for the participants. It also helped them do their jobs better the next day. This is a different model for learning based on different assumptions. And it works. CalState TEACH took learning to work and turned the workplace into a learning place. There is no reason why Troops to Teachers and other training and education opportunities as yet unimagined can't do the same thing.

Such approaches to learning are not only effective, they are efficient, using joint capital investment to implement because they use the workplace as the learning laboratory. With web support, they require no separate campus, no costly prepublished library of books, no artificial separations between working and learning. They literally reimagine and recast the educational uses of time, space, and responsibility.

Conclusion: New Practices and Policies Needed

To respond to the emerging need, higher education, business, and labor need to rethink their positions. Business will need to broaden its focus on profits and growth and its instinctive opposition to taxes and public-sector investments to include an aggressive human-capital, education-and-development strategy. A failure to invest adequately in our nation's human capital today will ensure even greater down cycles in tomorrow's economy. Employers also need to rethink their human resource development, training and education programs. An alliance between in-house training and education and the local college or consortium would allow employees to work toward degrees and satisfy elective requirements while developing their effectiveness at work. Learning could be web-supported, offered in the evenings, over lunch, or on the weekends. And a program that assessed work and personal experience for academic credit would bring the life and professional experience of employees into play as a form of advanced placement, tapping their existing knowledge.

At the same time, colleges need to become more accountable for the learning they generate and the capacity of their graduates. They can restate degree and certificate requirements in terms of results: the knowledge, skills, and abilities that graduates will have when they finish. This outcomes-based approach makes the standards public for all to see. It also requires the institution and faculty to align their teaching and assessments to each other and to the graduation standards. In workplace-related programs, outcomes-based curricula also provide the necessary quality assurance. With a web-supported, outcomes-based approach, colleges and institutional consortia can then enter the workplace offering programs that support the employees as well as the goals of the employer.

The stakes are high. If we fail to reform, American jobs and capital will leave for other countries in numbers and types we have not yet imagined. Unless we succeed at educating new and aspiring groups of citizens for new levels of professional skill, professional employment, and professional success we are and will remain at risk as a nation. We can pursue wars against terrorism and dictatorships, but the most fundamental battle we must win is that on which all others depend: the battle for learning that enables us to challenge all that breeds disease, poverty, ignorance, discrimination, and hopelessness.

By 2025, we will have two American wage earners for every one Social Security recipient if we stay on our current course. This will not work socially, civically, or economically. We will see economic decline at home, a widening gap between rich and poor, and an erosion of civic participation. These things will happen, not simply because of low wages, but because we have been out-taught, out-thought, and out-fought in this new battle. This is the national security issue of the early 21st century.

9

▼

FutureThink: Quality in the Learning Age

Steve couldn't believe his luck. Along with everything else, he had met the woman of his dreams. And while he was going to school at that! Now when they chatted about the work they were doing, he could put a face with her name, Sharea. And beyond any of the academic activities he was pursuing, pursuing Sharea had become part of his daily life.

His mind wandered back, looking for the critical moment where, if he had made another decision, he might not have met her. It was his visit to Dr. Gomes's office. If he hadn't gone to the educator's office—"Education Ltd, est. 2016, Dr. Duane Gomes, fully certified," the web advertisement had read—he wouldn't have met her. There, his educational advisor, Dr. Duane Gomes, had developed an educational program with Steve. He had started with a full diagnosis of his intellectual structure and intelligence profile. It had been a little frightening to Steve. What if he was just plain dumb? Or unqualified for the next step he wanted to take professionally? But Dr. Gomes had assured him that these diagnostics were designed to identify strengths and weaknesses so that they could be worked on, developed, and strengthened.

And that's what had happened. When he saw what his areas of relative weakness were, it explained so much to him. Why he had had trouble in high school and during his first stab at college. Among other things, he had been amazed to learn that he worked better in groups than alone, and that his visual and kinesthetic intelligences were very strong while his logical and analytical intelligences needed development. And now he could use college to strengthen those areas as he did the academic work. It had never occurred to him that specifically prescribed physical exercise and development could actually improve his academic performance, but it had!

The passport had also been invaluable. With all this information in his new passport, Steve had been ready to go to step two, an overall assessment of what he knew from college, the workplace, and his personal life. With that under his belt, Steve could take the credits awarded for his assessed learning and the outcomes he had addressed, along with his learning profile, to any participating employer in the region and have it accepted as evidence of his job qualifications as an applicant. He could also use it for advanced placement at any participating college. Issued by the Cumberland County Educational Cooperative (CCEC), the passport was part of the national passport program managed by the Learning Partners Service, a national nonprofit organization. The monthly service fee was a small price to pay for the support and security his passport gave him. The passport was like a ticket.

He had been relieved to find out that he qualified for financial aid, because it looked as if the whole sequence of studies that would take him through his BA to his master's degree would eat up at least three years and cost over $30,000, including Dr. Gomes's professional fees. His financial need was calculated as a voucher for qualified services, so he got to pick and choose how to use the money he qualified for, selecting from approved services and programs. Gomes had helped Steve get a handle on all this in his initial, complimentary counseling session.

Initially, Steve had been secretly worried when he and Gomes began to review the various options available to him for learning new material. His work schedule had ruled out the weekend colleges that had been so popular for so long. And he was too tired at night to drag himself out to one of the neighborhood centers where classes were available. And, anyways, that route took too long. He wanted to do it and get through it! It seemed like the web-based programming was his only hope. He could do it wherever he was thanks to his ubiquitous wire-card that gave him high-speed access to the I3 anytime and anywhere. And the chat rooms and hotlinks to experts and best learning resources made the support look pretty darned good. All the libraries were part of the resource bank, so he had support in that quarter also. Selecting any one of several sources for help with a problem—an expert, a faculty adviser, or an-

other student, among others—had seemed so practical. And the high degree of alignment between the material he was studying and the learning outcomes he was responsible for demonstrating gave him great focus while leaving him room for interpretation and creativity in developing his projects.

As he wandered the web-based aisles of the education superstore, Steve had weighed the various advantages and disadvantages of the many curricula offered. He read the critiques and observations of other users, faculty, and employers, providing insight and perspective on the value of the curricula available. They were all approved by the National Association of Accredited Programs, Services, and Institutions (NAAPSI), which meant that his financial aid was good for any of them and the credit could go on his passport upon completion. And he saw that they were graded for exit-level competence, identifying what he would know and be qualified to do if and when he finished each curriculum successfully. He just didn't want any buyer's remorse on this one. So, Dr. Gomes had been a big help, once again.

It seemed almost laughable that he had worried about the impersonal nature of it when he started. It seemed like a logical worry. All web-based, all the time. No human contact, except with Dr. Gomes from time to time for his regular advising and support sessions. But he hadn't anticipated the chat room and another student, Sharea, who seemed to engage him regularly halfway through his first project. And when she had suggested that they attend one of the monthly optional study sessions on Saturday afternoon, he had agreed, despite having to cancel his bowling match, because he was struggling a little with the work and a little coaching wouldn't hurt. It had, after all, been one of the reasons he had chosen this particular software package and curriculum.

Well, the rest was history. The expert coaching had been a huge help. But Steve had also come face-to-face with the woman of his dreams. And now, two years later, as he looked forward to graduation down at the CCEC pavilion, he rolled the engagement ring in his pocket and tried to muster the courage to ask Sharea to marry him. Remembering his mother's wry smile as she gave him the family engagement ring, Steve had to agree: Some things hadn't changed at all.

Web-based, advising-based, workplace-based; consortium-based, assessment-based, and community-based. Steve's campus is the community, including cyberspace. And the only place where his program adds up is on his passport, including his portfolio of work. How are we going to keep track of all of this? In a world of this complexity, where campuses are only one set of the service providers available, who is going to mind the quality store?

Outdated Conceptions of Quality

Quality assurance in the learning age will be a difficult and challenging task for colleges and for political leaders. Instead of regulating the flow of students into college, thus dealing with a preselected group of learners in a predetermined and controlled environment, we will reach out into our communities and workplaces and become successful with new students, in new places, learning in different ways. In layman's terms, we will educate a lot more people to high levels of quality in settings and circumstances that were unconceivable 25 years ago. As we understand and develop the new learning ethos, we need to build in quality with quantity.

Unfortunately, however, we begin this discussion with one arm tied behind our back. American higher education doesn't have an inclusive and broadbased definition of academic quality. When it comes to quality, as the character in Pogo commented, "We have identified the enemy, and it is us."

America has an historic confusion between academic access, academic quality, prestige, and status. For the most part, academic quality is not described in publicly stated standards. It is inferred, derived from the individual institution's reputation, the awards and achievements of the faculty, the prior academic achievement of the entering students, the size of the college's budget and endowment, the depth of the library collection, and, today, the quality and availability of the technology infrastructure. High-quality institutions are those that admit highly qualified students and then graduate them four years later. This is important work. But it is essentially a confirmation of young people who are already on an existing success track. The main task is to keep them going, not hurt them, and get them through to graduation. In this worldview, the more accomplished and successful your students are, the better an institution you are perceived to be.

This approach to quality ignores the more than 80% of America's colleges that work with students who have the capacity to learn but have not demonstrated significant educational accomplishment. These learners are considered to be less important, less prestigious. And the programs that serve them are perceived to be less qualitative even though they require better teaching in order to achieve success and, when successful, actually add significant value to millions of students' lives as well as to society's human resource base. This confusion about quality is widely shared but rarely discussed, making the problem even more difficult to confront and solve.

The Push for Accountability in the 21st Century

Recently, however, there has been increasing pressure from employers, educational innovators, and some political leaders to connect quality to performance and effectiveness, not anecdote and history. For example, parents, politicians and policymakers are concerned that spending on higher education has little relationship to quality and effectiveness. The overall results don't seem to change, regardless of spending. We serve more students, with more money, but we don't appear to be able to do it better or more effectively and efficiently. This concern represents a big change in the rules for existing colleges and universities. It trumps the historic value that higher education has contributed to American society, a value in which providing more of the same was considered a tangible and significant benefit, by asking an additional question: How well will we serve the needs of all learners in the 21st century?

As the education industry struggles with issues like this, the learning age is simultaneously changing the rules again, eroding the historic influence held over higher education by leading universities, national associations, and related businesses is in significant decline. Today, this assemblage of interests, dubbed the iron triangle, appears to be more like the Maginot Line as the changing needs, knowledge, and capacities of American society overrun them, redefining and pressuring traditional practices.

- Traditional universities no longer control the faculty workforce in post-secondary instructional settings through the PhD. The variety of instructors and instructional modes is increasing. It is common for qualified professionals to teach in their area of expertise.

- The privacy and primacy of the individual faculty member has been modified by teams of knowledgeable people, who working together, create web-supported curricula.
- Campus-based institutions no longer control the location of instruction, the supply of students, or the standards for graduation. Classes and online learning now dot the landscape with off-campus opportunities that, in turn, attract new students to the enterprise. Experiential learning can be assessed for academic credit.
- Degrees and certificates are increasingly available from new, nontraditional and alternative sources.

In this climate of confusion and change, we are called first to redefine quality and then be accountable for achieving it. Defining and achieving quality may be the single most difficult policy issue facing higher education. Currently, the debate sails between the Scylla of "bright line indicators" and the Charybdis of "we've always done it this way." Unfortunately, there are two big problems with these approaches:

- Neither is based on what we know about learning, assessment, and organizational effectiveness.
- Neither will deliver the quality, satisfaction, and confidence that we want from public accountability.

Bright line indicators are attractive to some policymakers. The idea that there is one test or one indicator that defines and represents quality has the great value of apparent simplicity and credibility. Taken alone, however, such indicators almost always lack the dimensions that good information provides about the learner's or the institution's overall capacity. They ignore the complexity of reporting on the results of high levels of achievement. And from a parent's perspective, bright line indicators provide no evidence about the noninstructional services or the quality of instructional processes needed to support the learners who are enrolled and get large numbers of them to graduate.

There is more to accountability than simply setting academic standards and asking institutions and students to live up to them with high-stakes tests. For example, if we only did that, employers would continue to be frustrated by recent graduates who had learned well how to recall information and give it back on tests, but who required retraining upon employment because they didn't know how to apply knowledge and continue to learn in the workplace. They want more Sam Hudnuts, Esther Jameses, and Steves.

On the other hand, the accepted academic disciplines and the historical assumptions about quality and standards—the marks against which our height is measured on the wall of public acclaim—are out of place in the 21st century. They may have been just right for an elite group in the 19th century. And they survived the 20th century. But the 21st century demands something more. For all the reasons discussed earlier, the organizational and academic model that has predominated in higher education will not be able to answer new learners' needs in the 21st century. It will become an important part of a larger, more diverse mosaic of academic services whose overall impact is to provide access to many more learners, retain them in higher education programs, and successfully graduate them into the larger society as socially, civically, and economically literate citizens of the 21st century. Consider the case of Margarita Sanchez.

Margarita could not believe the story she was hearing from her mother, Maria. Seated around the living room in her house after her graduation from Butte University (BU), her mom was telling her how she had finally gotten her degree, the first in the family to do so. And what a story it was! A leader in her worker housing collaborative in the late 1990s, a fighter for clean conditions, fair rents, and home ownership, Maria had been approached by representatives from the local community college who proposed to set up a learning cohort in conjunction with the state university just down the road. The cohort would initially build learning programs around the concerns of the residents, housing, governance, and child development; getting them their GEDs, associate degrees, and finally the BA. Meeting on Saturdays, the cohort slowly progressed, losing some members, gaining others, and supporting the learning right there in the community. When they were ready, some members began to attend classes at the community college and the university, receiving support services as they did.

"Ah," Maria lamented. "It was confusing and difficult. But I didn't want to depress you too much before you got your degree. They were good people, well intentioned. But we never knew what they wanted. We would discuss the issues, do the reading, and write the papers, but they never told us an example of good work, or asked us how what we were reading related to what we already knew. We were working blind, in a sense, with no clear view of the objective, other than finishing. And always, you have the teacher sitting there with the power to decide if your work is good enough to pass. It was like finding your way in the dark.

"Sometimes you would have 12 mothers sitting in a room with a college teacher who hadn't raised a child, talking about some aspect of child development, out of the book. And, as nice and supportive as they were, we never knew how far we could go in saying, 'It didn't work that way for me.' In the real world, the situations we faced were different. So often we kept our mouths shut and just did the work. We knew the point was to get the degree."

Margarita knew her mother had been a trailblazer in the community. But the program Maria described was as different as night and day from her recently completed program. For sure, Margarita had wanted support for her learning. She had survived high school, barely. First just staying in school when the classes went over 40 students in a room and the boredom was almost unbearable. But her mother leaned hard on her and told her to stay. And then managing to finish in the top half of her class. Not great, but better than dropping out, for sure! So, when it came to college, seven years later, she wasn't ready to strike out on her own, using the web and those advising services that were available, it seemed, on every street corner. She wanted a home, to be based at the university. It just felt better to her.

As she thought back over the experience, however, Margarita realized that from the moment she began talking with the university, she had always known the rules, what was expected of her at BU in order to be successful. They had a carefully designed intake process of counseling, advice, assessment, and support that never left her wondering where she was or what was coming next. And they were always asking her how they were doing, as well as telling her how she was doing.

The learning outcomes in each course and for the program were clear, but not restrictive. There was plenty of room for interpretation. And she had plenty of examples of good work to observe if she became confused about their quality expectations. And not only her prior knowledge, but also the way she learned had been respected, with an assessment and the development of her learning profile. She wasn't repeating things she already knew because the learning she had derived from her experiences as an administrative assistant and a paralegal were built into the base of her learning contract with the university.

With the learning outcomes clarified, the hard work was thinking and working your way toward them. That was plenty hard enough. And with your experience and prior learning recognized, you understood the connection between your past and your future. Finally, the development of her learning profile had been a real eye-opener! She had always known she was a talker, just like her mother. But to understand that as a piece of her intelligence, a way that she learned, had been a huge step.

Somehow, they had managed to take the fear and mystery out of learning, replacing it with the hard work and thinking that good learning required. The advising and support services that were provided by BU were on point and helpful. And the ubiquitous, asynchronous technology support was incredible. She could access the web, her friends, or her working partners at the touch of a finger. Knowing the rules made all the difference. And having a map of her path through the curriculum had allowed Margarita to focus on the important things: thinking, learning, and producing results. Now, she was heading to law school with her BA safely tucked under her arm. This was a long way from barely graduating from high school.

Accountability and Quality in the 21st Century

Quality assurance in the 21st century will rest on accredited institutional capacity, effectiveness and outcomes-based education. By 2025, we will embrace a wider and fundamentally different conception of quality that includes process- and results-oriented standards. Our standards will build up from learning outcomes for every student and around the institution's capacity and effectiveness—regardless of its organizational form—at adding value to a learner's life through education.

Accreditation and Institutional Effectiveness

Regional accrediting agencies have assured minimum standards and consistency in degree-granting programs for many years. Nothing can diminish the importance of this peer-review system. At the same time, few areas of higher education will be as challenged as the role of accreditation in assuring quality in an increasingly diverse delivery system where educational outcomes and institutional effectiveness are the determining quality factors.

Some associations are addressing these very issues. For example, changes implemented by the Western Association of Schools and Colleges (WASC) have created both a process and an environment to assess institutional capacity and effectiveness, hence quality. WASC's approach is outcomes-based and uses institutional portfolios. Simultaneously, the Council for Higher Education Accreditation (CHEA) has promoted new standards for accreditation and quality assurance of distance learning programs (CHEA, 2002). Both efforts will be useful in advancing the discussion about new forms of accreditation and quality assurance.

Both approaches suggest that in the future, colleges and universities will be assessed on their ability to educate for observable results and succeed at quality assurance reviews. Put another way, just as we will ask students and faculty to live in a results-oriented culture where evidence is critical through outcomes-based education, so will colleges and universities live in the same culture of accountability as organizations committed to learning. This culture of accountability and quality will include providing and documenting a learning process that is founded on quality standards. Any institution that aspires to be excellent—Stanford, Michigan, Monterey Bay, Phoenix, or Alverno—will be able to document and describe how their learning processes are effective at generating learning. American higher education needs a common and appropriate set of standards against which to measure our educational processes. And institutional effectiveness, as well as criteria and expectations for success will be public and publicly stated.

The National Survey of Student Engagement (NSSE), sponsored by the Carnegie Foundation for the Advancement of Teaching and the Pew

Forum on Undergraduate Learning, has produced one such assessment that is worthy of serious consideration by thoughtful policymakers (see http://www.indiana.edu/~nsse/). The NSSE's assessment is based on five national benchmarks of effective educational practice directly linked to research findings on the quality of teaching and learning. They can be applied across all learning settings to generate information about the effectiveness of the program involved. They can help all of us evaluate the presence of good educational practice in our undergraduate programs, thus getting a handle on how effectively we are educating students. The NSSE benchmarks emphasize the outcomes, the consequences of being involved in quality processes in higher education. If we are interested in the impact that our academic models, teaching, and support systems are having, the value that is being added to learners' lives through effective educational practice, benchmarks like those of the NSSE are far more accurate indicators of quality than grades alone, or the prior educational achievement of the learner.

Good practice, based on valid research, will contribute to better results. The sooner accreditation and quality assurance policy demands this type of approach, the sooner we will be hitting goals for equipping students to be lifelong learners. This will, however, require a quantum leap in understanding by most policymakers. They will need to embrace a new conception of standards; a commitment to organizational effectiveness; good practice; and results, graduation, employment and satisfaction. Stanford and Monterey Bay may well embrace different goals, based on a different vision of their mission. Vive la différence. This is the diversity of American higher education at its best. But the reputation of both should be based on the ability to succeed with effective practice that leads to good results, publicly stated, and related to the institutional mission. This way, we can define high quality as institutional effectiveness: the ability to meet objectives in learning and add value to the learner's life, separate from who the learners are and how they are served.

Some questions that would get at this approach to quality would include:

- What is the relationship between each enrolled student's rank in their high school graduating class, time to degree, and attainment of the degree?
- Does the institution employ demonstrable quality processes to support learners, learning, and quality assurance?
- How well do they work?
- How does the institution know?
- How many learners graduate? How long does it take them?
- What do they say about the experience?
- How well do they do after college?
- What do their employers say about their readiness to work?

This focus on effectiveness, capacity, and learning outcomes is coming just in time. Our understanding of quality, of what good curriculum is and what it means to be well educated, will continue to develop in response to the market for learning. For example, one scholar, Ada Demb (2002), has suggested that part of the learning infrastructure of the future may be modeled on networks of retail outlets. Think of web-based learning libraries as something akin to a supermarket. According to Demb, then, it might look like this:

- Products are treated as commodities with minimum standards for quality with competition occurring on the basis of price and perceived quality differences.
- The supermarket is largely self-service.
- The supermarket does not take responsibility for the customer's diet or overall health—it merely offers a fantastic array of goods for the customer's choice.
- Customer safety and capacity for judgment are supported by related regulation and markets [such as] the FDA and state health departments.

Certainly, the variety of new providers entering the marketplace [of American higher education] has dramatically increased. And the federal government is moving incrementally toward complete portability of financial aid, including the proprietary context . . . Yet the supermarket analogy highlights at least two assumptions, fundamental to the structure of the current system, that must be questioned and examined before new models of higher education can be established. First is the assumption that the responsibility for a student's educational experience and progress properly rests with the educational provider rather than with the student; and second is the assumption that individual instructors create better learning experiences (i.e., course materials) than do groups of faculty or course designers. (Demb, 2002, pp. 20–21)

A simpler example of the new infrastructure is MERLOT, the Multi-Media Educational Resource for Learning and Online Teaching described earlier. Already widely available, MERLOT is the product of an international cooperative of educational institutions. It makes online curricula available to faculty and learners alike via the World Wide Web. It is an early model of a curriculum structure that exists separate from traditional universities, waiting for learners and other entrepreneurs to claim its educational value and the enormous market potential it symbolizes. It is a short step from the library of material to an institution supporting the use of that material in organized learning programs.

Quality will increasingly become a consequence of institutional effectiveness, of achieving outcomes, of value added to lives. Higher education will be seen as successful when we are as inclusive as possible and when we can succeed to high, publicly stated standards with more students. These will include the new traits called for by business leaders today: the ability to work in teams, to apply high-level knowledge in a diverse array of settings, to communicate effectively, to reflect and think critically across different circumstances, to employ technology, to work across cultural differences, to learn throughout life, and to respond as educated people to the challenges that life generates.

The policies governing accrediting agencies' standards and expectations must also be changed along the same lines: capacity-based, outcomes-based, learner-based, effective. Future policy should encourage the accrediting associations and colleges to worry less about issues like the test scores of incoming students and the size of the library and more about the institution's ability to consistently employ quality learning processes and continuously evaluate its performance; employer ratings of alumni learning and performance; and the institution's capacity to generate successful learning to high standards in many students.

Specifically, there are six areas where the policies supporting accreditation need serious discussion.

- All institutional evaluations and reports should be public. The public has a right to know and the institution has a responsibility to be accountable.
- Accreditation should focus on assessing the capacity and the effectiveness of the institution, on how well it does, not solely on what it has.
- All accreditation should rest on the ability to deliver a clearly articulated outcomes-based curriculum and manage continuous improvement and quality processes.
- Distributed learning, web-based or other, must be welcomed with open arms. The issue should be effectiveness and quality assurance, not the mode of delivery.
- Accreditation must become a consistent national process with consistent standards that are managed through regional agencies. It is not acceptable for this country to have variable standards in different regions in an age of global communication and great population mobility.

- The explosion in special interest accreditation groups must be understood and controlled.

Some might argue that the primary objective of improved accreditation is to give the government and the taxpayers better information and control through accountability for the investment they make. Although that is a legitimate and important objective, I would argue that it is secondary. Quality assurance is not the end, it is the means. Improved accreditation and quality assurance should lead to improved educational results for learners, employers, and society. Government got into the business of supporting higher education because we had the best system in the world and because we understood it to be the gateway to opportunity. Our current system is successful by any measure. The issue before us is not the dismantling, but the expansion of vision and purpose to accommodate a new age. Higher education needs to renew its focus in response to the new forces in our society. But the focus should be clearly on effectiveness at the institutional and individual learner level. You cannot regulate your way to excellence.

Needed: A New Level of Institutional Quality

The goal of higher education accreditation policy should be to improve the quality of learning and our institutions' ability to demonstrate these improvements. Improving the basic quality-assurance program with policies like those that WASC has adopted will create a new commitment to excellence and continuous improvement in higher education.

We need, however, to take another step. How will the students of the 21st century know if their institution is truly superb? As discussed earlier, prestige and status today are conferred on the institutions that have long histories, huge endowments, and well-prepared incoming students. In the future, being in the elite should indicate that the institution adds significant value to the learner's life, a very different standard. Developing this new standard will require a now-unrecognized higher level of quality recognition for institutions aiming to become the new elite during the 21st century.

An effective first step in this direction would be an elective, second tier of national accreditation that operates a full level above the existing regional levels. In this conception, current accreditation would become a basic assurance that the institution achieves appropriate quality for the learning age. But an advanced level of recognition, modeled after the Baldridge Award and based on effectiveness research such as the National Survey of Student Engagement, would reward an institution that fully achieves high standards as a learning organization. Because the initial level of accreditation had already been achieved, thus assuring the basic quality of the institution, this advanced level could be elective—pursued at the institution's choice—and confidential— without the potential embarrassment associated with failing to achieve the higher quality standard.

The introduction of such a new, higher recognition would democratize status and prestige, giving all colleges and universities an opportunity to demonstrate and be rewarded for high levels of effectiveness and organizational quality. Capacity and effectiveness at adding value would lead to reputation, not the other way around.

In the learning age, a reputation for quality will be earned every day. Deep resources and rich tradition will always be part of the mix. But they will be seasonings compared to the bulk of the recipe: excellent teaching and learning, publicly stated standards and objective assessment of learning, access for people of all ages and cultures, appropriate technology, responsiveness to the needs of learners, and the value-added to the learner's life through education.

Conclusion: Major Leadership Shift Needed
For the leaders who find themselves burdened with the challenges and thrilled with the opportunities that higher education in a learning age will bring, I echo the suggestion of a higher education leader who was intimately familiar with challenges and opportunities, the late Clark Kerr: "The major test of a modern American university is how wisely and how quickly it adjusts to important new possibilities" (qtd. in Keller, 1983, p. 40).

The changes in policy and practice required for improved accreditation based on institutional effectiveness and capacity will not succeed without a major shift in leadership attitude. Critical standards are implied through the value statements our leaders make. They are shaped by the policymakers, sometimes within our communities but often at a great distance; by the chancellors and college presidents whose imprimatur is required year by year and campus by campus to win political truces; by the seasoned professionals who haunt the associations and councils of higher education where excellence is too easily bantered about as coin of the realm; and by the journalists who write and comment on higher education. Therefore, it is with a sense of personal admonition that I recall David Riesman's (1980) bold and proper wisdom: "There has always been room for innovation and fresh starts in American higher education, even if this freedom, which rested partly on expanding enrollments and funds, is more circumscribed now. What is really lacking is strong and visionary leadership" (p. 164). We need it now, across the board.

10

▼

FutureThink: A Policy Framework for the 21st Century

In Chapter 3, I used the *Titanic* as a metaphor. It's a dramatic image, maybe a little much, but I think it fits. Think about it for a moment and ask yourself, what is the greatest single problem you associate with the *Titanic*? An arrogant captain? The iceberg? A longer view suggests that even if the *Titanic* had survived her maiden voyage, she was doomed. The iceberg, the captain, and the disaster that occurred only confused the situation. The real problem facing the greatest cruise ship ever built was the airplane. The seeds of destruction for the ocean travel industry had been sown a decade earlier in Kitty Hawk. Cruise ships could not compete and attempts to make them competitive ultimately failed. Almost a century later, the cruise ship industry is geared to luxury travel aimed at relaxation, not necessary travel with speed.

As a college president, perhaps I face the risks of an arrogant captain. We have the greatest higher educational system ever developed. People travel from around the world to attend our colleges and universities. And the annual scramble to get into our top institutions is becoming evermore contentious because of the value associated with getting a degree from them. Economic and social icebergs challenge our course. We must anticipate and navigate dexterously to survive.

But the icebergs we face aren't our long-term problem. The greater risk is that the potential of the ships we sail is—because of their basic design—limited, and therefore fundamentally outmoded. They are being eclipsed by new need, new knowledge, and new capacity.

We face a situation in which doing more of the same—creating new campuses, growing our existing campuses, expanding degree programs, all our stock in trade since World War II—is not sufficient to the challenges we face. Any one of three forces—demographics, knowledge, or technology—can, on its own, make the case for significant change in our academic enterprise. But the interplay of all three creates a synergy of need and capacity that will not be satisfied by extensions of our traditional approaches.

Needed: A New Truman Commission

Following World War II, there was a time of uncertainty in American higher education that was, in many regards, similar to today's looming crisis. Flush from victory over fascism and state socialism, faced with potential economic and demographic turmoil with returning troops, President Harry Truman convened a group of national leaders to make proposals for the future of higher education in America in 1947. Seen by some as a political ploy, the Truman Commission stunned American legislators and university presidents with a set of policy recommendations that redefined the debate about the meaning of higher education and access to college.

The Truman Commission estimated that at least 49% of the American public possessed the native ability to complete 14 years of schooling, including two years at the college level. The authors also believed that a third of all Americans had the capacity to obtain a four-year college degree (President's Commission on Higher Education, 1947). Remember: This was 1947 when institutional and structural racism and prejudice still jaundiced the vision of our nation's true potential. Even so, the Truman Commission re-imagined the possibilities for higher education and for America, making recommendations that revitalized and dramatically extended America's system of higher education.

Just as in 1947, the current policy assumptions and core values for higher education were developed in response to a world that no longer exists. A different economy, mostly regional and occasionally national, was in place. Definitions of teaching and learning, of what constituted success for students and faculty, of who should be admitted and how they should be educated—all were geared to ideas and realities now long gone. For the last half century, we have been growing beyond the policy assumptions that govern higher education, making them increasingly irrelevant to the world around them. It's time to shake loose from the image of higher education as mainly a campus-bound, two- or four-year experience for America's best high school students.

We need a new consensus, this time on the role of higher education in the 21st century. America is on a learning curve to its future, propelled not by design but by swirling forces unleashed by our knowledge and our growth, by our successes as a beacon of freedom, and also by our shortcomings. If we are to lead the world into a "Knowledge Century," we must commit to giving all qualified Americans the opportunity to succeed through education, including higher education that gives them the ticket to opportunity. This will require a revolution in our thinking. Harnessing the power for this revolution is the number-one policy challenge in America today. We can carve and follow a course to our nation's potential, a national learning plan for the learning age, or we can continue to be swept along on a rising torrent of social, intellectual, and technical change, like a wood chip in a raging river.

Think again of the challenges we face and the opportunities we hold: the inalterable demographic realities of America, the frozen model of higher education that we've retained, the revolutions that have occurred in understanding human learning and expanding worlds of technology. Then imagine what a 21st-century version of the Truman Commission might propose.

Here are some assumptions and core values that I would suggest for the next Truman Commission.

DEMOGRAPHICS TELL THE TRUTH
Most college learners will not be white and young. The American demographic landscape is changing around us. We wade through a flood of statistics, year after year, demonstrating the many ways in which we first enroll and then fail to serve Hispanics and African-

Americans and Native Americans and new immigrant groups as well as a large number of low-income Anglo students. The cost in economic terms is astronomic. The cost in social terms, where we continually widen the gap between those served by our tradition and those cheated by it, is unfathomable.

TRANSFORMATIONAL DEVELOPMENT OF TECHNOLOGY
WILL CONTINUE
Textbooks and classrooms will only be part of the picture; PCs and the Internet are here to stay. Learning can and does occur everywhere, all the time, for people of all ages—if they have access to and the ability to use technology. No college or university can any longer imagine itself as the repository of knowledge. Technology means we need not leave our workplace to become learners. Technology enables us to learn before the bells ring and after the school doors have been locked. Technology does not care whether its user is Muslim or Christian, eight or eighty, wealthy or poor.

AMERICAN EMPLOYERS AND WORKERS RECOGNIZE THEIR
NEED FOR MORE AND BETTER EDUCATION
Already employers expect that aging within our workforce will create more jobs (35.8 million) than will economic growth (22.2 million) (Hecker, 2001). What is terribly uncertain is how a younger, more diverse workforce will be equipped to replace those now in place—and what institution will take on the challenge of effectively equipping them. But now we know how human beings learn most effectively. We know that learning is done best when it is personal and experiential, organized by learning projects and following the learning cycle. We know how to encourage learning, and how to discourage it. We have the knowledge we need to build new and effective models of education at all levels. Given what we know in the learning age, our 500-year-old tradition of higher education is outmoded.

Needed: New Core Values for Policy and Practice
Making good policy is a difficult business. I've been involved in education policy for over 30 years. I've served in elected positions at the local,

state, and federal levels. And I've worked at the local, state, and national levels in program and policy development. Too often, the tendency is to control, to direct, and to limit the scope of activity through a new policy initiative. As we reform college policy and practice to respond to the new learning ethos, however, we need academic leaders, corporate and business executives, community champions, and policymakers at all levels to adopt some new core values. They include:

- A climate that rewards change and experimentation
- Creating new partnerships in the delivery of postsecondary education
- Enhancing the delivery of postsecondary education in a global, learning age
- Supporting active and engaged learning pedagogies
- Rethinking financial aid
- Reviewing institutional accreditation policy and practice

REWARD CHANGE AND EXPERIMENTATION

First, we must be committed to a climate that rewards change and experimentation. We do not want deadening sameness across our curricula or our colleges. America is diverse and so should its colleges and institutions of higher education be diverse in form and function. Policy should focus on results and quality processes, on learning, not teaching. A standard approach to teaching or learning won't serve us well. But high standards for results and quality processes will.

Policy should encourage a culture of innovation, improvement, and quality assurance for colleges and universities that enable all students, regardless of age, ethnic background, or environment, to succeed. We need to encourage individuals and organizations to create new learning forms, based on what we now know about how people learn, because America will need continuously revitalized learning strategies. If we spend these early years in the learning age resisting reform, we will waste not only our time but also our nation's opportunities. So, what are some areas needing reform?

If the government does not support educational research, it won't happen. No private-sector corporation can step in to provide equivalent focus or support. Yet, while the government provides $122 million in direct support for such research, it is a pittance compared to other research investments. We spend 74 times more money on health-related research at NIH, nearly 24 times more money at NASA. We have, as a nation, not believed that investment in educational research and innovation was necessary. Now, better, more focused research and development is critical.

An area ripe for research and public investment is the development of an affordable, accessible battery of assessments that allows institutions—colleges but also employers and other nonprofits and for-profits—and individual learners to know individual learning profiles. It would be the equivalent of the basic health information doctors collect during physicals. It would tell how each of us learns best. With the technological capacity we have, this information would follow the learner through life.

Such work is already underway, sponsored by pioneering organizations such as Bridges Learning Systems (www.bridgeslearning. com) where broad-based assessments are routinely used to define individual student learning profiles. The resulting improvement in retention and learning rates is significant.

Bill Brock, former United States senator and now Bridges Learning Systems' CEO, has compared learning to seeing, that it is a natural or instinctive activity. He notes that most testing in today's educational systems are intended merely to determine a student's progress. In fact, he argues, we should measure a student's ability to learn and the learning style that best fits her or him. Given the current approach, says Brock (2001), when a student is failing, instead of seeing how we are failing the student we

> . . . buy new textbooks, we jazz up the curriculum, we change from whole language to phonics, we employ new computers, we do everything we can to adjust the externals we control. And, when all else fails, we beat up on teachers and we beat up on children . . .

As parents, we never, never would treat our sick children the way we treat children who struggle in school. If you and I had a child with a 103-degree temperature, a bad stomachache, cold sweats, and tremors, never would we think of suggesting "come on Billy, you're not trying hard enough to get well." We would take him to the doctor, find out what was going on, and have it fixed.

Senator Brock's assessment is correct. But because we pass along our failures in most educational systems, or wait for them to drop out or walk away, the system we have devised protects not the students but the systems themselves. We've built in the belief that students, not systems, fail. These failures most often go directly into the workforce carrying with them the belief that they have now failed into work.

At the same time, we must recognize that efficiency and effectiveness are essential components in the public's partnership with higher education today. We must be efficient because we don't have unlimited public or private resources. We must be effective by using the latest science of learning and the latest technology that serves such learning for each individual student. The objective of public policy should be to put the resources, the knowledge, the incentives, and the accountability into the hands of our students and institutions, asking them to identify their best way to serve learners and to continuously improve their performance.

And, as research is completed, the Fund for the Improvement of Postsecondary Education can become the primary link for developing models that apply research results and develop new education delivery models. It may be that the fund's purpose can be underscored and its role in this debate can be enlarged by virtue of an even clearer focus on the goal of supporting the results of applied research to drive program development, and innovation. We must focus especially on applying the benefits of learning research in communities that have not traditionally enjoyed the benefits of higher education, communities that lack economic vitality or large population bases, or both. Technology and distance learning open new opportunities for these communities and, therefore, for all of us. We need to seize the opportunity to meet their needs.

CREATE NEW PARTNERSHIPS

Second, we must be committed to creating new partnerships in the delivery of postsecondary education. Our policy vision must extend beyond the federal government to our state houses, chambers of commerce, teacher unions, school boards, neighborhood centers, and corporate boardrooms. Higher education will no longer be the province of a few; it must become the common territory for nearly all of us.

Partnerships that link curricula to the expressed learning needs and interests of students will generate active, community-based learning. Senator George D. Aiken of Vermont is always remembered for his shrewd resolution to the Vietnam quagmire: "Declare victory and bring the boys home." But in his home state, and throughout New England, he is still revered as the person who fought the private electric companies until he brought affordable electric power to the end of every Vermont dirt road. He did it by establishing electrical cooperatives where ownership was shared and the customer was boss.

We need educational cooperatives dedicated to supporting college learners and learning. Educational cooperatives would allow small and large businesses to pool their resources and support learning for employers, suppliers, and customers. Museums, hospitals, local governments, and other nonprofit, community-based organizations would also qualify. Cooperatives would act as brokers for some educational opportunities and as providers for others. They would all be learner-friendly and community-based. Federal, state, and accreditation policy could nurture such cooperatives with funding, with status and with technical assistance.

And who might work in an educational cooperative? Just as colleges and universities will take on new roles in the learning age, so will the professionals who serve in new programs. New alliances, like cooperatives, will need newly trained professionals to staff and operate them. Professors will still be needed, especially in certain fields and types of institutions. So will counselors and administrators and facility engineers. But new, critical higher-education professions already are emerging: technology experts, individual assessment experts, and community services experts. We haven't invented the titles and job descriptions, but already I can imagine a host of new professional roles.

The professional educator might combine the skills needed for assessing and diagnosing learners and learning, and for creating learning programs that bring them together. Professional educators could be coaches, sources of learner support, advocates, and problem-solvers. They might be the guarantors of outcomes and the certifiers of quality. The American League of Educators (ALE), a society of such professionals, would form. It would set the criteria by which professional educators qualify the workforce, identify best practices, and devise a code of ethics for its membership.

Finally, America's personal learners need an educational passport; a place to bank their learning whenever and wherever they do it. Soon, standing alongside other nonprofits that serve America's institutions will be a new educational service that serves America's personal learners. It will house a national assessment and credit-assurance program that allows any learner to receive diagnostic assessments creating their learning profile as well as a cumulative, continuing appraisal of life experience and formal learning anytime and anyplace. This credit assurance program would be student-centered, outcomes-based, and quality-assured. Its outcomes matrix could well become a voluntary set of national indicators for college learning outcomes.

Enhance the Delivery of Higher Education

Third, we must commit to developing policies that enhance the delivery of higher education in a global, learning age. This will go far beyond mere reauthorization of previous acts even though the Higher Education Act itself can be a critical vehicle for change. Congresses and administrations come and go. But it is imperative that they, together and consistently, redesign our federal partnerships in ways that enhance and promote virtual learning—anytime, anyplace—across our nation.

Personal learners—at work, at home, and in their communities—are the largest target of opportunity for educators and entrepreneurs today. They are hundreds of millions of friends and neighbors, cousins and colleagues, waiting for learning support services that will assess what they know, organize their learning, help them learn more, validate their learning, and enhance their lives.

As a nation, we have to add more value through education. There are two population groups currently unserved where significant potential for added value is possible: people with untapped potential and people with untapped knowledge.

People with untapped potential are those who disappear from our schools and colleges before graduation. They have the capacity to learn and to contribute, but do not persist in either school or the workplace that typically follows. Business leaders have been telling us for some years that the dramatic change in the face of our nation's demographics will lead to an equally powerful change in the face of our nation's workforce. With 65% of all jobs requiring postsecondary education—a number that is increasing daily—we must engage a commitment in higher education to leave no person behind because economic development in a high-technology, global economy requires engaging business in the design and delivery of lifelong, workplace-based education.

People with untapped knowledge have capacities that are already developed but which remain unrecognized because the credentials given by higher education have been withheld from them. They need to have their knowledge assessed, to gain advanced placement for what they already know. These are the Peg Moores and Connie Yu Naylors of America. I've seen no data assigning an economic cost to untapped knowledge but it is enormous. We lose what they know and have to offer and we also lose the opportunity for them to learn more. Social justice, if not economic interest, compels us to open doors to their greater economic success, higher standards of living, and greater contributions to society.

As long as we exclude these people from higher education, we promote a de facto policy of national bankruptcy. We can count the dollars we are squandering. According to the Educational Testing Service, we entered the 21st century forfeiting nearly a quarter of a trillion dollars every year as a result of our failure to educate Hispanics and African-Americans alone (Burn, 2002). They are among the populations full of untapped potential, untapped knowledge, remarkable skills, and vast capabilities, all largely ignored or turned away by our traditional models.

SUPPORT FOR ACTIVE LEARNING

Federal and state legislative bodies can encourage reform that supports active and engaged learning including service-learning. Serving our communities is the seed corn of democracy as well as a powerful pedagogy that has been tested and proven in the field. Experiential learning makes the learner wiser. Service-learning makes the community stronger. When service-learning happens, communities are stronger and learners are wiser. When it does not, we all suffer silently. People in need languish and the souls gathered at the country club are just a bit drier. A national policy on service-learning is a critical element of the learning age.

Imagine if every college in America established accredited, required service-learning programs and 50% of federal college work-study funding were allocated to service-learning. This change alone would revolutionize the experience of higher education for students and for every American community. And rather than constraining the university's budget, it would connect the school with its community. Transitioned over three to five years of implementation, it is a reform that every college should readily embrace.

We can also support other established forms of service to the community with academic recognition. This learning experience would be paid for by learners who themselves receive public funds. When learners have the power of cash, institutions will rapidly become more accountable for learning. For example, California State University–Monterey Bay, in cooperation with the Leon and Sylvia Panetta Institute for Public Service, recently joined four other colleges to offer credit for VISTA/AmeriCorps service. In doing this, we are simultaneously reducing the financial disincentive that operates against low-income students who would like to serve their country while linking civic engagement to college-level learning.

Using the community around the college as a learnplace as well as a workplace will also rebuild the ethic of community service in

America. Throughout our history, civic engagement at all levels, from local politics to simply doing good deeds and helping out, has infused the American spirit. In his trips across a younger America, Alexis de Tocqueville was astonished at the nature and the depth of the values he encountered. He wrote with awe about the uniquely American instinct to form voluntary associations to solve problems. He understood that within this volunteer impulse to serve, to solve, and to contribute lay the resilience of the society. It is one of the ways that, as a society, we breathe, inhaling good will and solutions while exhaling shared problems and pain.

Robert Putnam (2000), in his provocative book *Bowling Alone*, argues that we are practicing less community than ever before. Families no longer gather as regularly at the evening dinner table and attendance is declining at service clubs. In these and many other areas where community used to be affirmed, Putnam claims that our participation is declining precipitously. Today, people appear more inclined to talk in chat rooms with folks they've never met and socialize with people at work than they are to attend a community meeting to discuss water quality in the neighborhood.

Although higher education is not the culprit leading to the demise of community, neither has it offered many solutions. We have been too distant from our communities, too eager to think we exist for our own higher purposes rather than the community's urgent needs. But there is an educational consequence to this posture of divisiveness and distance as well. By standing apart as ivory-tower institutions, colleges have not only abdicated their moral responsibility as leadership institutions and deepened the divisions between communities and institutions; they have also weakened their academic programs and lowered their quality. Civic engagement is, after all, not only a national instinct and strength, and a part of our moral code; it is also a source of powerful learning. In the learning age, both diversity and engagement will be key quality indicators for colleges.

RETHINK FINANCIAL AID POLICY

Fifth, federal and state policymakers need to thoroughly rethink financial aid policy. The federal government provides more than $12 billion annually in student financial assistance, and the private sector adds some $1.3 billion (The Foundation Center, 2002). Despite this largesse, tens of millions of citizens are barred access to higher education for structural and financial reasons. The availability of the money, the terms on which it is offered, and the structure and circumstances of their lives do not align with the offer that postsecondary education makes. We must not simply think about ways to increase financial aid and reduce the cost of higher education, but we must look at the barriers that lie between potential learners of capacity and the promise of education.

Equal opportunity, national interests, workplace education, lifelong learning, web-based programs, accreditation standards—if we rethink the role of colleges and universities in the learning age, we must be willing also to rethink the financial consequences of this new role. For a fact, more portability for financial aid is a necessity. But who should receive the aid? And where, when, how, in what amounts, for what purpose, and with what expectations? Recent studies have suggested that the major barriers to college completion for poor and minority students involve their inability to maintain four to five years of consecutive study. If they stop-out, they are less likely to re-enroll. Financial aid policy should include incentives to achieve graduation equity for the students who initially enroll in college.

We cannot avoid redirecting the largest student-aid program in America, Pell Grants. Low-income students and communities, in particular, suffer debt loads that may have been tolerable in an earlier economy, but are not in the current one. Similarly, the one grant per calendar year and other provisions slow down the pace at which working students can complete their degrees. Again, the burden falls disproportionately on those students with least financial resources, greatest need, and, tragically, greatest motivation. We have a system that literally challenges the spirit of those with whom we need most to make a difference.

ACCREDITATION POLICY MUST BE REVIEWED

And finally, accreditation practice and policy must be seriously reviewed. American higher education accrediting agencies, practices, and standards have assured consistency in degree-granting programs for many years. Nothing can diminish the importance of this peer-review system. At the same time, accreditation will be challenged by an increasingly diverse delivery system where educational outcomes and institutional effectiveness are among the determining quality factors.

The goal of higher education accreditation policy should be to improve the quality of learning and our institutions' ability to demonstrate these improvements. Any program that offers degrees and credits to the American public should have basic accreditation. Improving the basic quality-assurance program with policies like those that WASC has adopted will create a new commitment to excellence and continuous improvement in higher education. This is a critically needed step.

Another step needs to be taken, however. As described initially in Chapter 9, American higher education should develop an elective tier of accreditation that is a full level above the existing regional and national levels. Being considered among the best should be connected to evidence that the institution employs best practices and adds significant value to the learner's life. Accreditation as we now know it would become a basic assurance that the institution achieves appropriate quality for the learning age.

The advanced level of recognition, modeled after the Baldridge Award and based on effectiveness research such as the National Survey of Student Engagement, would recognize institutions that fully achieve high standards as learning organizations. The introduction of such a new, higher recognition would democratize status and prestige, giving all colleges and universities an opportunity to demonstrate and be rewarded for high levels of effectiveness and organizational quality.

Conclusion: Centers of Learning, Not Teaching

Our nation has long held to the premise that business, academia, and government are all necessary stakeholders in the common mission of teaching, research, and service. Today, our colleges must become centers of learning, not teaching. And Congress must become as committed to research into education as they are to research for health care or space exploration. They must connect the dots properly between national education and national defense. Therefore, we must all find ways amid limited resources and intense competition to reshape higher education to broader and better definitions of service.

The Quiet Crisis was written in recognition of these challenges. I hope it contributes to a thoughtful discussion. So let us follow our new learning curve as parents, politicians, leaders in higher education and business, and as a nation. We see the forces gathering in our communities. We live with the inventions enabling change and the knowledge of how learning occurs. And we have the capacity, the skills, the obvious needs and the unleashed aspirations. In the years ahead, these forces will intensify, broaden, and deepen. To succeed, America needs a new road that leads to a learning society for all Americans, bringing their traditions and cultures, their hopes and aspirations to the table of opportunity. Alan Kay, the personal computer pioneer, offered the sort of wisdom that needs to permeate higher education and those who set the policies that shape it: "The best way to predict the future is to invent it."

Bibliography

Adelman, C. (1999). *Answers in the toolbox: Academic intensity, attendance patterns, and bachelor degree attainment.* Washington, DC: U.S. Department of Education. Retrieved December 31, 2003, from http://www.ed.gov/pubs/Toolbox/index.html

Adelman, C. (2000, May/June). A parallel universe: Certification in the information technology guild. *Change, 32*(3), 20–29.

Altbach, P. G., Berdahl, R. O., & Gumport, P. J. (Eds.). (1998). *American higher education in the twenty-first century: Social, political, and economic challenges.* Baltimore, MD: Johns Hopkins University Press.

Astin, A. W. (1993, March/April). Diversity and multiculturalism on the campus: How are students affected? *Change, 25*(2), 44–49.

Belenky, M. F., Clinchy, B. M., Goldberger, N. R., & Tarule, J. M. (1997). *Women's ways of knowing: The development of self, voice, and mind* (10th ed.). New York, NY: Basic Books.

Brock, W. E. (2001, September). *Focus on each child.* Paper presented at the Education Leaders Council, Phoenix, AZ.

Burn, B. B. (2002). *Expanding the international dimension of higher education* (Business–Higher Education Forum). Washington, DC: American Council on Education.

Cairncross, F. (1997). *The death of distance: How the communications revolution will change our lives.* Cambridge, MA: Harvard Business School Press.

California State University. (2002). *Systemwide evaluation of teacher education programs in the California State University 2002 (second year).* Long Beach, CA: Author. Retrieved December 31, 2003, from http://www.calstate.edu/Teacheredeval/Eval_ExecSummary.pdf

Carnevale, A. P., & Fry, R. A. (2002). The demographic window of opportunity: College access and diversity in the new century. In D. Heller (Ed.), *Condition of access: Higher education for lower income students* (pp. 137–152). Westport, CT: American Council on Education and Praeger Publishers.

Collins, J. (2001). *Good to great: Why some companies make the leap . . . and others don't.* New York, NY: HarperCollins.

Council for Higher Education Accreditation. (2002). *Accreditation and assuring quality in distance learning* (CHEA Monograph Series 2002, No. 1). Washington, DC: Author. Retrieved December 31, 2003, from http://www.chea.org/pdf/mono_1_accred_distance_02.pdf?pubID=246

Daloz, L. (1982). *Radicals.* Unpublished manuscript.

Demb, A. (2002, July/August). The intellectual supermarket. *Educause Review, 37*(4), 13–22. Retrieved December 31, 2003, from http://www.educause.edu/ir/library/pdf/ERM0240.pdf

Dewey, J. (1916). *Democracy and education.* New York, NY: Macmillan.

Drucker, P. F. (1999). *Management challenges for the 21st century.* New York, NY: HarperBusiness.

Flint, T. A., & Associates. (1999). *Best practices in adult learning: A CAEL/APQC benchmarking study.* New York, NY: Forbes Custom Publishing.

The Foundation Center. (2002). *Distribution of foundation grants by subject categories, circa 2000.* Washington, DC: Author. Retrieved December 31, 2003, from http://fdncenter.org/fc_stats/pdf/04_fund_sub/2000/10_00.pdf

Fulbright, J. W. (n.d.). *The global Fulbright legacy.* Washington, DC: Fulbright Association. Retrieved December 31, 2003, from http://www.fulbright-jordan.org/profile.html

Gardner, H. (1983). *Frames of mind: The theory of multiple intelligences.* New York, NY: Basic Books.

Gilligan, C. (1982). *In a different voice: Psychological theory and women's development.* Cambridge, MA: Harvard University Press.

Green, M. (Ed.). (1989). *Minorities on campus: A handbook for enhancing diversity.* Washington, DC: American Council on Education.

The Greystone Group. (2001). *Visions for UW-Stout's future.* Arlington, VA: Author.

Handy, C. (1989). *The age of unreason.* Cambridge, MA: Harvard Business School Press.

Harrington, M. (1962). *The other America.* New York, NY: Macmillan.

Hecker, D. E. (2001, November). Employment outlook: 2000–2010: Occupational employment projections to 2010. *Monthly Labor Review, 124*(11), 57–84. Retrieved January 2, 2004, from http://www.bls.gov/opub/mlr/2001/11/art4full.pdf

Heldrich, J. J. (2002, February 20). *Standing on shaky ground: Employers sharply concerned in aftermath of recession and terror.* New Brunswick, NJ: John J. Heldrich. Retrieved January 2, 2004, from http://www. heldrich.rutgers.edu/Resources/Publication/59/Standing%20on%20 Shaky%20Ground%20PDF%20Final%20Report.pdf

Jones, R. T. (2002, Summer). Facing new challenges: The higher education community must take the lead in addressing the dramatic pace of external change. *CrossTalk, 10*(3), 10–11. Retrieved January 22, 2004, from http://www.highereducation.org/crosstalk/pdf/ct_summer02. pdf

Keller, G. (1983*). Academic strategy: The management revolution in American higher education.* Baltimore, MD: Johns Hopkins University Press.

Kretzmann, J. P., & McKnight, J. L. (1997). *Building communities from the inside out: A path toward finding and mobilizing a community's assets.* Chicago, IL: ACTA Publications.

Kuhn, T. S. (1962). *The structure of scientific revolutions.* Chicago, IL: University of Chicago Press.

Meeker, M. (1969). *The structure of intellect: Its uses and interpretation.* Columbus, OH: Charles Merrill.

Meister, J. C. (2001, February 9). The brave new world of corporate education. *Chronicle of Higher Education,* p. B10.

Mishel, L., Bernstein, J., & Schmidt, J. (2001). *The state of working America 2000/2001.* Ithaca, NY: Cornell Press.

Mortenson, T. (2002). *ACT institutional survey, NCES–IPEDS graduation rate survey.* Boulder, CO: The National Center for Higher Education Management Systems. Retrieved December 16, 2003, from http:// www.higheredinfo.org/dbrowser/index.php?submeasure=119&year= 2000&level=nation&mode=data&state=0

National Center for Education Information. (1998). *Profile of troops-to-teachers.* Washington, DC: Author. Retrieved January 2, 2004, from http://www.dantes.doded.mil/dantes_web/troopstoteachers/profile-text.htm

President's Commission on Higher Education. (1947). *Higher education for American democracy.* Washington, DC: Government Printing Office.

Putnam, R. (2000). *Bowling alone: The collapse and revival of American community.* New York, NY: Simon and Schuster.

Queeney, D. (1996). *A learning society: Creating an America that encourages learning throughout life.* Washington, DC: The Kellogg Commission of the National Association of State Universities and Land-Grant Colleges.

Riesman, D. (1980). *On higher education: The academic enterprise in an era of rising student consumerism.* San Franscico, CA: Jossey-Bass.

Senge, P. M. (1990). *The fifth discipline: The art & practice of the learning organization.* New York, NY: Currency.

Sheckley, B. G., & Keeton, M. T. (2001). *Improving employee development: Perspectives from research and practice.* Chicago, IL: Council for Adult and Experential Learning.

Sheehy, G. (1976). *Passages.* New York, NY: E. P. Dutton.

Smith, P. (1986). *Your hidden credentials: The value of learning outside college.* Washington, DC: Acropolis Books.

Staple, G. C. (Ed.). (1995). *TeleGeography 1995: Global telecommunications traffic statistics and commentary.* Washington, DC: TeleGeography, Inc.

Swail, W. S. (2002, July/August). Higher education and the new demographics: Questions for policy. *Change, 34*(4), 15–23.

Tough, A. (1971). *The adult's learning projects: A fresh approach to theory and practice in Adult Learning.* Toronto, Canada: Ontario Institute for Studies in Education of the University of Toronto.

U.S. Bureau of Labor Statistics. (2002, September 19). *Employee tenure summary.* Washington, DC: Author. Retrieved December 31, 2003, from http://www.bls.gov/news.release/tenure.nr0.htm

U.S. Department of Education, National Center for Education Statistics. (2001). *Digest of education statistics 2001.* Washington, DC: Author. Retrieved January 2, 2004, from http://nces.ed.gov/programs/digest/d01/

INDEX

DATE DUE

AP 10 05			
I LL			
1248826			
10/27/05			
MR 2 1 09			

DEMCO 38-296